HOLY *but* THEOLOGICALLY UNEDUCATED

JOCEPHUS BINGHAM SR.

ISBN: 979-8-89031-586-1 (sc)
ISBN: 979-8-89031-587-8 (hc)
ISBN: 979-8-89031-588-5 (e)

One Galleria Blvd., Suite 1900, Metairie, LA 70001
(504) 702-6708
1-888-421-2397

"Lack of knowledge destroys people. I cannot associate with those who reject the pursuit of knowledge. You'll no longer be a priest to me. If you forget God's law, I'll ignore your children, too," Hosea 4: 6.

CONTENTS

INTRODUCTION

Are you excited about your Christian faith, or do you feel as if you are merely going through the motions of what you are supposed to do as a believer? Are you walking by faith with confidence toward your goal, or do you feel like you are going through the motions without a clear mission or destination?

Do you recall when you were so enthusiastic about Christianity? But now, the zeal has faded, making you question: What has changed? So, the doubts come. Why do I feel so listless and unmotivated by my righteousness? When I reflect on my local church, personal life, and the global situation, why do I only find one or two things that bring me delight and optimism? Then you wonder what has caused your central motivation to disappear.

People recognize patterns that repeatedly appear, and these questions can perplex them. For instance, focusing on the negative aspects of a situation will keep you stuck in that frame of mind. You may not even notice it. This is why in Philippians 4:8-9, the Apostle Paul urges us to fill our thoughts with good and holy things. Furthermore, Jesus' foundational teachings encourage us to live by Divine grace, not our own strength.

2 Timothy 1: 9 tells the readers THE LORD invites Christians to a sacred mission out of His intention.

But often, most churchgoers are unaware of the distorted doctrine. To stay conceptually errorless, the writer constantly compares what he thinks; to what the Bible says. His convictions provide a framework for living a life devoted to righteousness. For instance, Biblical dogma has stood the test of time, endured through the ages, and remains relevant or helpful for this generation. Joecephus is awestruck by the Bible.

Inconsistency arises when individuals misinterpret the Bible. Then, they insert their opinions and beliefs based on their upbringing, experiences, and culture. They have no other choice but to spiritualize their faith. The irony is they cannot answer questions about the meaning of life. Or how THE LORD interconnected humanity, the universe's true nature, and other puzzles of humankind's existence.

Surmising Christian Doctrine triggers our boredom when Church worship does not suit us. For example, one might feel bored because the songs or hymns were not to their liking. So, they are uninterested in Church service to the point of weariness. Yet, the Bible is exciting to read and listen to, with stories full of bravery, love, and salvation. Still, others find reading challenging because it is difficult to understand and interpret.

And then, they criticize the Holy Orders as uninspired, unenjoyable, and boring. But when one follows the Scripture, it leaves no room for boredom when contextually shared. Even though they wrote the Bible thousand years ago, like any other ancient book void of the Holy Spirit, it is difficult to understand by anyone who can read. The Bible is unique from every other book because the Master of the Universe inspired it. The Holy Spirit is vital in our Bible interpretation. God breathed out the Bible. (2 Timothy 3:16). So, every moment we follow the Scripture, all praises go to Jehovah. Hence, there is never a dull minute for Christians.

The author disparages no part of the worship service. Prayer services, hymns, praise songs, etc., are essential. Yet, Psalm 30 11 says, "God's Word turns our mourning into dancing."

So, when anybody gets to the point, they cannot go any higher in righteousness or do any better in the redemptive cause. Then, they usually feel inadequate or unprepared to witness their faith. They have forgotten the feeling of joy that salvation activities used to give them. Still, others say they feel plagued by their lives—stuck in their circumstances, wondering what it is all about. What is my life's worth, or what happened to my joy? Doctor Bingham's book Holy, But Theologically Uneducated, can help you see life from God's perspective.

Often, Christians live what the writer calls a settled-for mundane faithfulness. Someplace along their righteous journey, they became complacent and content in their worship circumstances. They settled for what they believed was satisfactorily worshiping. But the Apostle Paul described true worship perfectly in Romans 12:1-2: present our bodies as a living and holy sacrifice. And prove what the will of God by knowing the will of God.

For instance, when we were in grade school and got good grades, we shared our scores. Yet, we never went around telling everyone about our bad scores. The teachers graded us with three words: outstanding, satisfactory, or unsatisfactory. Here is the unhealthy rub for Christians; if we become satisfied with a reasonable effort of Bible understanding, we are unlikely to strive for superiority.

Contentment with mediocrity worship will rarely spur a person to strive for excellence in their faith. Completing routine tasks to achieve satisfactory outcomes is what they expect. When confronted with material wealth, those lacking confidence can become easily intimidated. At last, they leave their commitment to THE LORD and decline to aspire, seek, or strive.

If that is where you are today, I encourage you to study the chapters of this book to see yourself as God sees you. Examining yourself from a Divine viewpoint will cause you to rise above the complacency of your everyday life and strive for more.

Correctly reading the Bible is essential to life, as it is God's way of communicating His plan, love, and message. It steers us on the right path, shows us to Jesus, and boosts our trust. Too, memorizing Scripture is an effective way to study the Bible alongside our daily Bible reading.

CHAPTER 1

HOLY BUT THEOLOGICALLY UNEDUCATED

The Christian Bible is a bestselling publication comprehensively. Yet, even mature theologians often misinterpret the Messiah's Sacred Writ! So, how can anyone read the Book of Books with understanding? Jocephus' question is rhetorical: Scripture is the means of comprehension. But we should study it properly, allowing the content to interpret the context.

To extract the most profound meaning from the text, the Saints should allow the circumstances to confirm the historical analysis. Specifically, it means following the story or message to expand their thinking and fulfill God's goals. Our understanding of Biblical truth should echo the Scripture.

For instance, with any manuscript, we must follow the principles and processes of research and applicability. Looking at how the technique works and then using it to address real-life problems needs to happen. For example, who drafted it, under what conditions did they write it, and how can it benefit this temporary culture?

The Bible has influenced history, art, engineering, and journalism. Although secularism publications have billions of stories we can read, lacking the complete picture. But the Holy Scripture narrative gives you a much greater awareness of literacy and goes further than one's beliefs.

God's Word reveals how men inspired by the Almighty wrote about Jesus, to everybody, His greatness, and goodness. The Scripture brings spiritual growth into our lives by telling us about the predominant sovereignty of the Creator. The pages of the Holy Writ show us the Nature and Character of God.

Scrutinizing the Scripture helps bibliophiles understand its relevance today. Reading this Ancient Consecrated Book cultivates physical and spiritual growth.

Holy, But Theologically Uneducated will support how to understand the Bible. Assisting the reader in grasping the Bible's message. Every individual's message remains the same: "God sent Jesus (His Son) to save and re-create all that has fallen and broken." So, the Bible is relevant because salvation to Heaven and damnation to Hades are as accurate today as 2,000-plus years ago.

Specifically, Christianity is based first on repentance, faith that JESUS CHRIST is God, and then He forgives our sins. It is impossible to learn morality when someone uses their religious belief to mask wrongdoings instead of confessing them to God. The Saints should prioritize finding a Bible-teaching Church. Then, pray for the ability to remain and withstand the urge to leave when encountering issues with parishioners and leadership.

No one who is an uncommitted trustworthy searcher can find authentic righteousness! The senseless parishioners of the Church aimlessly wandered from one place of worship to another, their curious ears always on the alert. But without a commitment to blameless irreproachability in the Son of Jehovah the Redeemer, there can be no Christian way of life.

Hyper-faith Christians cling to misguided beliefs to ward off conversion. So, they choose not to focus on evangelism but as a substitute for the condition to get results in economic well-being. Thus, they wander around for religious sermons to make them feel happier. They accept lies instead of the truth of faith's teachings.

Further, facing the Sacred Text causes pain to undecided members. Faithful Christians know them as Church hoppers. These vacillating Saints have misconceptions surrounding themselves. They trust they are powerful and in control because of their excellent upscale life extravaganza. We should never allow what THE LORD has blessed us with to go to our heads. If He blesses us with innumerable funds, pray and wait a couple of months before making any financial decisions. And doing that time, list what you would like to accomplish with the money.

The false doctrine, name it and claim it or 'Blab it and grab it,' opposes finding their place in an unembellished trustworthy congregation. Rather than finding a spiritual home, they travel from Church to Church. They seek sermons, teachings, and messages that will give them a false sense of validation for their erroneous beliefs. These people are looking for instructions that excuse their sins. See Second Timothy chapter Four.

But the Bible tells us to set our mind and heart to seek the Lord our Holy Father. (1 Chronicles 22: 19). Since Christ raised us with Him, we must seek the things above, where Christ sits at the right hand of the Supreme Being. Righteousness is a conscious choice that causes us to set our minds on things above, not on things on earth. (Colossians 3:1–2).

Contrariwise, you should NOT feel guilty about your rich portfolio, lovely home, and the nice cars in your driveway. These are a blessing from God because of your hard work. God wants us to enjoy the fruits of our labor and have delightful things if what He blesses us does not get between Him and us. We should continuously try to deepen our relationship with the deity; hence, righteous magnification must be paramount.

Specifically, we should always seek to grow in Christ, foremost. So, read a chapter or two from Psalms before prayer to enhance your faithfulness to God. Share with others what you are receiving in a non-threatening manner. Try to attend a small group Bible study. Then pray for understanding and ask the Holy Spirit to help you understand life from God's perspective.

CHAPTER 2

THE BIG LIE

The origin of misguided fact dates to Lucifer's time in Eden when he asks Eve, *"Did God say?" Genesis 3: 1.* His three words questioned the Almighty's meaning.

However, Eve makes mistakes that most people make. Instead of being thankful for the natural beauty and the hundreds of fruit trees they could enjoy in Eden, she focuses on the one simple thing THE LORD told her not to do. Then she presupposes that God needed her help by adding her supposition to what God said about the forbidden fruit: "Neither can we touch it, lest we die" (see Genesis 2:17, 3:3). The problem with lies multiplies into more lies.

Satan is our enemy–his goal is to lead us away from God. Therefore, we must never forget sin turns us away from God. Even if it is an untruth, we are trying to justify or prove it reasonable. And that happens when we add human supposition to THE LORD'S Word or about anything.

Satan artfully presented his deceitful words to Eve in a lethal, yet enticing, manner. Causing the first mother to doubt God's command, Satan's words entertained the possibility that God did not know what was best for them. But they soon discovered there are only catastrophic consequences when we reject God's Word as the only authority for our lives.

Although akin to a black hole, Satan's counterargument: *"Did God say?"* His misleading lie is still sucking the true intent out of the righteousness of uncommitted supporters. Unfortunately, the faithful principle makes the Saints righteously accessible to the Gospel veracity. John 8: 32. The Greek meaning for "truth" is living honestly. Then, taking control of the original Word of Christ will lead to freedom. In our daily ways of life, the truth can set us free. So, surrender your thoughts to the Messiah, and watch Him bring to light increasingly of Himself to you.

But the *false gospel* has an inauspicious heart-changing effect on the disciples. He cautioned believers to watch out for false prophets (Matthew 24: 24-25, Matthew 7: 15). Bogus philosophy is after the fashion of accepting a fatal disease in one's life. Likened to Lou Gehrig's Disease, it begins painstakingly inactive, yet gradually weakens and destroys the body.

Disingenuous teachers slowly but deliberately steer Christians away from Christ. The Saints must shield themselves from conflicting teachings. False teachers prey on illiteracy, apathy, and gullibility. To withstand inconsistent Dogma, speak the Word over your lives and to everybody around you. It is a matter of make or break. Eiji Yoshikawa said, "The line between life and death is not thicker than an eyelid." Yet the writer of Proverbs warns: Death and life are in the tongue's power, and those who love it will eat its fruit (Proverbs 18: 21).

Any information not honoring Christ comes from a seducing spirit. Yet, humans accommodate secular knowledge. So, for Christians who live according to the flesh, anybody's spellbinding false doctrines can mislead them.

Heresy is why THE LORD wants His people to have a wealth of sound dogma. Heterodoxy is after the fashion of death from a thousand cuts. Every unorthodox thought is a strategy for unrighteousness to prick other souls. It hurts the person who receives it and then passes it on to massacre other righteous spirits. Alternative religion turns the Glory of God into a lie.

Reading and studying the Scripture supplies an abundance of God's enlightenment in every part of living in Holiness. Hence, when someone teaches something new, your Holy Spirit will at once recognize unsoundness. So, the more we study the Divine Writ, we will know teachings that do not match what is in the Hallowed Scripture.

The Authoritative Book confirms and crystallizes the importance of reading Scripture. It dispels the lie that one needs a theological degree to help with the Word. Jocephus Seminary training is invaluable. But his independent Bible study enabled him to grow closer to God and dispel the lie of Satan, claiming: "There is no benefit in reading the Sacred Writ." However, the Scripture builds your Christian faith and affects the brain by affirming righteousness. So, what seems like a little lie from Satan is holistically detrimental.

When someone tells a minor lie, they can become more accustomed to telling larger and more complex lies. And that sets the stage for narcissistic behavior. For instance, erroneous teaching is the same as yeast spreading through the whole dough batch! The fungus searches for sugar, releasing carbon dioxide and alcohol as it eats. Immorality enslaves Christians. Bringing on diseases, divorce, home breakage, separations, etc., and afterward, death (Romans 6: 23).

Christian indistinct carnality can dominate their temporal desires. The residue of the normal anatomy is a reprehensible nature known as "living organisms." From a theological context, the old sinful disposition is "inconsistent with the Divine Spirit" (see Galatians 5: 17). The Word shows disciples that physical development and the Absolute Being are opposing forces living in the disciples of JESUS CHRIST. Therefore, we must seek the Spirit of Truth because Jesus is the Way, the Life, and the Truth (John 14: 6). He is the only way to the Father, as the Holy Spirit leads us further along.

We can see that the (Presence of Truth) transforms God's people. Without Christ's Comforter, the human carcass cannot respond to His righteousness. So, the inhabitants of The Paraclete point the Saints to serve the true Supreme Being in love and faithfulness. The Messiah sent the Breath of the Almighty to live inside those who accept Him as LORD and SAVIOR. He shows us the truth. Jehovah's fruit manifests in the Saint's lives as we walk by The Spirit, not the physical nature (Galatians 5: 16-22).

For instance, the disciples kept falling asleep when JESUS wanted them to pray with Him in the Garden of Gethsemane before His crucifixion. The Messiah cautioned them, *"The Paraclete is willing, but the flesh is weak" (Matthew 26: 41).* Jesus said to the Teacher of the Jews, "The flesh produces muscle and fat, but the Spirit gives life" (John 3: 6). So, an individual can be conscious physically (in the physical nature) but lifeless spiritually. But believers whose Holy Spirit has redeemed are alive righteously (study Ephesians 2: 1 and Colossians 2: 13).

The old and new spirits within the Saint create different desires. The former disgraceful sin residue consistently grows to torment THE LORD'S people to do the ungodly instead of being thankful to God. After they surrender even the smallest vile, that unrighteousness is more dangerous than serious offenses. We must battle the flesh daily to win this war (Romans 8: 13-14).

Noticeably, there are no modest trespasses. Christians may see specific transgressions as inferior to others, except every immoral act is wrong in God's Supreme Eyes. So, what we believe is insignificant wrongdoing is meaningful to God. We may think of a minority of injustices as "small" unethical behavior. And yet, THE LORD knows them as grim disobedience confrontationist to His commands. A perfect example of so-called minuscule sins is in the stories of King David. 2 Samuel chapter 11-12, Psalms 32, and Psalms 51.

Christians accept untruthfulness when they think the truth will make them vulnerable. So, they fear the consequences of evaluating its infallibility in their lives after hearing it. Then, when the facts materialize, they sense betrayal and lose faith in their ability to conduct sound judgments. So, even the trivial lies that fit into the minor misdeeds are dangerous.

Accepting unrealism can destroy families. Yet, we hang on to the untruth, since fallacious lies are more accessible for us to believe than to have our thinking changed by the Gospel revelation. Hence, we justify the nonsense in our hearts.

For example, in the Book of Judges, "Every individual believes the big lie that they could do whatever was right in their eyes." (Judges 17: 6). But believing lies pushes recklessly at an individual faith and kindles the flames of insatiability to want more sin. Then, the untruths disturb one's inward equanimity.

CHAPTER 3

DOES GOD RULE? THEN WHY DOES HE TOLERATE EVIL?

The evidence that the Supreme Being is alive and has all the ruling authority over His creation is objective realism. For instance, every theological forethought has a deeper Spiritual meaning to the quality of being right in the eyes of THE LORD. The Divine Essential Characteristic is the natural state of the Prime Mover and is, therefore, the opposite of man's sinful nature. The Supreme Being puts up with sinfulness because He is affectionate, merciful, and kindhearted. But He promises wickedness will not go unpunished and overlooks nobody's sins.

The Lord strongly dislikes six things and finds seven abominations; these include haughty eyes and a lying tongue and hands that shed innocent blood. One that plots wickedness with a crafty heart, hastening to do evil with their feet, is a liar of a false witness and sows discord among the parishioners. Proverbs 6: 16-19.

Having a righteous concept is the only way humans can accept The Father. Thus, a thought about divineness represents the mental condition of perfection, sanctified and set apart. The Word of Jehovah reveals He is not a superstition for grown-ups but an unimpeachable reality. Holiness is not human conceptual; it is God's standard; He is the Ultimate Lawgiver (Isaiah 33: 22).

Devoid of the Mastery of THE LORD, we would not exist. Opposite to the contention of skeptics and cynics throughout the epochs, humankind cannot live without the Supreme Being. Humans may have a mortal lifestyle, not accepting the Head of the Church, but not in reality's absence of Him. Even the atheists on their dying beds call out to God.

The Master's authoritative writings show His sovereignty. His connection with humans is graceful and vibrant.

The Book of Books holds that God is the Supreme Being, as stated in Genesis 17:1. Human predictions cannot override the Father's absolute authority. Tho, they can help us understand Christ's perfect Holiness. A true prophet of God, He calls to deliver His message to others. In Matthew 7: 16, Jesus says, "We shall know them by their fruits."

So, true pursuers of Holiness will find and know the superpower of the Messiah when they are open to how THE LORD works through His Word. But His Divinity is absent from disbelievers to prove Himself to any pagan groups of unbelief in Him. Righteousness is the prudent management of His assets and Christian Doctrines.

Colossians 2: 9 highlights God's authority. People's lives improve when they discover God, testifying to His greatness. Inviting Him into their lives, they lived virtuously. Holiness convinces them that God lives, reigns, and rules peacefully over His creation.

The cosmos follows the laws of gravity, physics, and energy because of Jehovah's design. Therefore, the Supernatural Being holds the universe together: And He [Jesus Christ] is before everything; by Him, all elements have their existence. Colossians 1: 17.

Conclusively, suggesting that objects and life happen without a cause is irrational. Such as homo sapiens, animals, insects, plants, the historicity of Jesus's resurrection, and the big bang theory are inclusive. That everything comes from an explosion implies incompetence. Atheism is the belief that there is no higher power. And Pantheism, that the Creator is " in all and" everything is divine. Thus, both concepts have no human or theological evidence to support them.

The evidence is that electricity, gravity, and air exist. A logical inference stipulates that either an entity or someone caused it. We can rule a thing out of the ordinary and use unique qualities as the answer. Since this would leave us with the same problem—what was the origin of the fundamental particles of matter or energy?

There is no guesswork regarding God's rules; this demand that the FIRST CAUSE (Cosmological Argument) is the uncreated ORIGINATOR. He then is the PRIME MOVER, which has always existed (eternally). We need not understand how this is possible, but it is reasonable to apprehend that it must be so because of Objective Morality or (Moral Dispute).

From the beginning of human inception, THE Lord implanted the difference between right and wrong in humankind. He told Adam and Eve not to eat from the "tree of knowledge of good and evil in the Garden of Eden."

But the evidence shows the foundational parents knew the truth from inaccuracy, yet still sinned. They did not run to God, begging for forgiveness; they immediately hid from the Almighty. So, their offspring grasp the distinction between faithfulness and wrongdoing without instruction. Specifically, people have an innate sense of integrity. That comes from a Righteous Lawgiver, whom we recognize as The Absolute Being.

God's decisions and reasons are beyond our comprehension. Deuteronomy 29: 29.

The world recognizes General Relativity, which Einstein developed as a helpful concept. It says that matter, space, and time intertwine all three and co-exist. The Bible does not contradict his theory; it proves that timescales and concurrent events are not preeminent. But God is absolute since He is immutable.

Therefore, He is relative to the extent He is temporal, having potentiality in His Holy Nature. However, the Most High reveals Himself by what He brought into existence. The first three verses of Genesis explicitly express all the known perspectives of creation.

"In the beginning, the Heavenly Father created the heavens and the globe. Now the earth was formless and empty, darkness was over the deep surface, and the Spirit of Jehovah was hovering over the waters. And He said, "Let there be luminescence, and there was light."

Thermodynamics explains radioactivity's use as a raw material. In the universe, for instance, there are substances and energy merged. There will never be extra of either and not any less. And both may achieve and assimilate into distinctive forms. Matter from nuclear power or exerted force into any substance that has mass and takes up space. But not these things existed before the King of the Ages created the beginning.

Yet, whether sincere or for argument, a handful of unbelievers say, "It's impossible to prove that the Divine Being exists." But it is ludicrous to think trilliums of atoms and sub-atomic molecules could materialize into existence from nothing. Is it likely that random particles alone formed the universe? So, most people know of the Designer-Creator (God); therefore, they rarely request proof of Him.

It is reasonable to prove God's sovereignty and existence by studying the law of sound judgment, specifying whether something is or is not. Saints testify to transformation through a relationship with the Holy Spirit.

Scripture On God Rules

Revelation 11: 15, John 3: 16, Revelation 20: 6, Colossians 1: 13, Ephesians 5: 5, Galatians 5: 21, 1 Corinthians 15: 24, Romans 14: 17, Acts 14: 22, John 18: 36, Matthew 6: 33, Daniel 2: 44, Revelation 21: 3, Revelation 17: 17, Revelation 5: 10, 2 Peter 1: 11, James 2: 5, 2 Timothy 4: 18, 2 Thessalonians 1: 5, 1 Thessalonians 2: 12, Ephesians 2: 6, 1 Corinthians 15: 50, 1 Corinthians 6: 9-10, 1 Corinthians 4: 20, Romans 16: 26, Romans 1: 1-32, Acts 19: 8, Acts 8: 12 John 18: 37, John 3: 3-5, Luke 10: 11, Luke 10: 9, Mark 10: 23-25, Mark 10: 14-15, Mark 9: 47 Mark 4: 26, Mark 4: 11, Mark 1: 14-15, Matthew 13: 38, Matthew 13: 31, Daniel 7: 13-14, Psalm 72: 1-20.

Why Does God Tolerate Evil?

Immoralities are the most perplexing problems in the Evangelical Church. However, these aggressive, belligerent attitudes exist in every Christian home and Worship Center. So, why would the All-Powerful Supreme Being allow the ungodly to thrive? Irresponsible Saints focus on their own needs and wants instead of ministering properly.

Still, we can only provide an underlying concept for moral wrongs. For instance, there is more than one definition of provocative behavior. When expressed in the adjective form, it means profoundly immoral and outrageous. But applied as a noun, it describes overwhelming immorality and wickedness. The noun also regards supernatural, cold-hearted force, evil-suffering, and the most egregious sin.

Sinful behavior, harm or destruction, and pointless hardship are all connected. But historically, the evil one periodically used the praise of morally wrong to justify individual torture and to rack on the Saints with pain. However, this prompts us to ask a crucial question.

Why could God not cease these evils since He has unlimited power? Yes, the Almighty is the Architect and Sustainer of the universe, and He can do anything He wills that agrees with His Righteous Nature. Without Immanuel's plan, the totality of creation would never have happened. And devoid of Infinite Spirit sustained operation, it will elapse.

Jesus is not only All-Powerful but Eternally Good, which makes the complication of evil puzzling. God could have stopped all transgressions and suffering by not creating us. Then, eliminate the same by allowing the universe's operational sustainability to end.

The Author of Life would end demonic/wicked acts and discomfort. But because He does not, it causes doubters to contend that THE LORD either does not exist or He is not Omnipotent.

Regardless, Jehovah's righteousness, purpose, or capability is authoritative. His Omnipotence attributes Him with infinite competency, overall sustaining eternally and in every way. He controls everything, from the smallest to the greatest.

So, The Head of the Church (Jesus Christ) can green-light evil for two reasons:

(1) Immoralities do not threaten or compromise Him. THE LORD'S power is too immense for Satan to intimidate Him with his immoral wrongs. His righteousness is too significant to allow iniquity to degrade it. He is The Atoning Sacrifice for humanity's sins. His boundless capability is more potent than human evilness, just as the most isolated stars are beyond human reach.

(2) The Author of Salvation is patient. Thus, His graceful disposition allows sinners space to atone or feel apologetic about their misconduct. So, THE LORD tolerates iniquity for each person to put their faith in Jesus. And God is eternally faithful to those who seek Him. When somebody "Repent," the Holy Spirit grants them peace and comfort, affirming their faith in the

> Almighty. Therefore, "Repent" denotes transgressors, turning their minds from immorality to enthusiastic righteousness.

However, feeling remorse for wrongs does not mean an individual does not do evil things—that is not the consequence of repentance. A resolve to change the unrighteous, to think righteously, alters the heart and its determination to discontinue sinning and not to sin, as in Philippians 4: 6-8.

"In times of trouble, do not allow troubles to overwhelm you—instead, go to the Good Shepherd with your prayers and petitions. And give thanks for all that you have. And the peace of THE LORD, which transcends all understanding, will guard your hearts and minds in Christ Jesus. Consider what is honest and good, what is beautiful and pure, and what is praiseworthy."

Again, The Supreme Being pours goodness and kindness into the Saints and the sinners, allowing them to repent. And if they do not act with deep regret or remorse, they have something in their life they will not quit that The Almighty hates.

As seen in Genesis, chapter 15 contains a brief account of the Amorites that moderately clarifies why the Holy and True do not condone wickedness. The passage tells us about the lifespan of Abram. But foremost, the reader understands Christ's interaction with the man of faith that four hundred years is a day in the Divine Being's eyes. Jehovah is not oblivious to evil people, despite Him being THE LORD of GLORY, which proves His tolerance as humankind continues in unholy deeds.

As we look at unscrupulousness in this culture, it is easy to be uncertain where The HEIR of ALL THINGS is. Remember that His sense of time and patience are distinct from humanity. Even though narcissists believe they have the air of being much the same as the Mediator of the New Covenant. They are the worst atrocities motivated by short-lived romantic ideals. So, from the King of Kings' perspective, He did not tolerate the sin of the Amorites. Too, He sees the immoralities of this society and will manage them His way on His timetable.

Therefore, understanding the Infinite Spirit's calendar is flawless. And Psalm 18:30 tells us: As for the Offspring of David, His plan is superb: His WORD is Preeminent; He shelters all who receive refuge from Him. Also, see Galatians 4: 4. Holy's action efficiency is never too soon, and He has never been late. Before we take the first and last earthly breath, our Unlimited Yahweh is accomplishing His primary Divine strategy.

There is no guesswork about the rulership of the All-Knowing, sovereign power. And by adhering to His Statutes and implementing them, humanity could have the most vital chance of survival. It is not enough to be a hearer of the Word; we must follow through and be doers.

Jesus said, "If we love Him, keep His commandments" (John 14:15). The ALL-MIGHTY does not want lip service but the heart and life obedience. THE LORD of GLORY set His LAWS with correct wisdom and absolute assurance that His plan is the top choice. He knows what is around the blind corner and has left us with His instruction manual, the Bible, to face it.

CHAPTER 4

THE KEY TO CHRISTIAN CALMNESS

Stabilized self-assurance is the greatest and most valuable treasure a believer can discover. The innermost peacefulness is a deep sense of spiritual unity or serenity. A Saint with inner tranquility feels alive and lives for the now, not bothered by past or future troubles. So, no matter the situation, a quiet spirit does not lose composure, whether the circumstances are welcome, unwelcome, or harmful. Their disposition remains calm and unruffled. Supporters of salvation find contentment and live in harmony.

No human mind could ever unearth authentic serenity in this life until they reconcile with Immanuel. It is why the Apostle Paul calls for the Saints to "Let the reconciliation of Christ rule in their hearts" (Colossians 3: 15). What does this mean? The tranquility arises from the Son joining the Father and humankind in unity and restfulness. Agreement with the Supreme Being creates peace. So, we cannot spread peaceful harmony and Gospel awareness to others if it is not within us.

Our LORD said, in John 14: 27: "Calmness I surrender with you, The truce I offer to you; not as the world gives, do I present to you. Troubled not your heart, neither let it be afraid. I leave you to love; I give you, My Friendship." Interpretation, a disciple, could be close to death, amid uncertainty, or inhaling the pressure of theological controversy. Yet, their soul shall not fail its inward peace, nor the strength of the infinite stillness of God.

Supporting one another through Christian Education unites us. Not all have found peace through the Redeemer in Scripture. Mutual respect facilitates understanding. Compassion comes from understanding suffering. So, clothe yourselves with Christocentric compassion.

John 4:20 states: You cannot love God if you hate your brother. Too, One Timothy 5: 8 tells us, "If any give not for his own, and especially for those of his own house, he has denied the faith and is worse than an infidel."

Followers of Christ are to follow His example: He served and did well during His earthly days (Acts 10: 38). Whenever JESUS came across a need for individuals or multitudes, His interest inspired a prompt response of compassion.

For instance, He fed, restored, instructed, calmed stormy oceans, cast out demons, and even raised the dead. Christ did and spoke to set a pattern for His adherents to follow to live a peaceful life through the ages (1 Peter 2: 21). FIND TIME TO FOCUS ON YOUR PURPOSE (HOBBY), AND JESUS WILL ADD THE PEACE (MATTHEW 6: 33).

He who does not have Christocentric harmony with the Almighty cannot experience the tranquility of the Holy Spirit. Their minds create a negative outlook that prevents them from enjoying the present. It causes them to overthink and dwell on what is instead of what is coming. So, without righteous soundlessness, one over-analyzes or over-scrutinizes every condition and communication. Thriving in the past can lead to stress, restlessness, and depression.

Further, do not allow the mind to wander over someone else's mistakes. It could stop the Glorified from forgiving themselves or somebody else. That means reliving painful memories. When anybody dwells in the past, they live in it, making contentment challenging to detect. Happiness comes from focusing on THE LORD as the Absolute Great High Priest to whom we must submit. But our society would have everybody believe that pursuing everything other than the Holy and True will satisfy us. Thus, humanity is searching hopelessly for joy by seeking material things.

Proverbs 12: 17 tells the readers, "Whoever speaks the truth gives honest evidence, but a false witness utters deceit." So how does one discover this self-actualization? And how does one combat the deceptions and return to untroubled calm and peace? Each disciple must confront misinformation about their righteousness for peace. Plant their feet solidly on Holiness after slipping, stumbling, and falling for untruth. Within Jesus Christ's teachings, we realize His plan for our happiness.

Believers can approach life's challenges with Christ's teachings. They choose tranquil righteousness over sinful habits. To exemplify, comply with what life demands. Or hold the fortitude to stay dedicated to Devoutness through your mortal existence by being your authentic character in Christ.

Too, fake stories pose a severe threat to the Christian nation. Negative connotations and the secular broadcast media can manipulate the most conscientious Christians. Studies have shown that multitudes of Americans cannot tell what articles are false and what news is trustworthy. Therefore, we must seek "THE LORD" for calmness and truth. The Bible says Jehovah is close to all who call on Him," declares the Psalmist (Psalm 145: 18).

Untruthfulness will create unpeaceable misunderstandings around significant, social, and faithful connotations. But if the Glorified wants to reach their fullest potential in peaceful development, they must believe what the Good Book says they are. Psalm 139: 14 makes the well-known statement, "God fearfully and wonderfully made His

Saints." So, reading Sacred Writings regularly and consistently has countless benefits.

First, the Holy Writ shows the readers THE LORD'S Character and provides the person who reads with peaceful revelation. Second, in each section of the Sacred Book, we see God's Sacredness, unchanging, faithful, gracious, and Loving Personality. Thus, it encourages individuals to be mindful of the thoughts, words, and actions they decide.

Scripture teaches us how to be transparent and trustworthy in our transactions. The Saints can be themselves and need not force their presence on others, pretending to be someone they are not, fearing people will not accept them. The act of constructing hypothetical situations triggers anxiety. Fearful people avoid confronting their true selves. They have difficulty intellectualizing their feelings, so they absorb other people's emotions. Jesus crafted His Saints fearfully and marvelously.

So, never tolerate negative thoughts of the past to define you. And do not allow preexistent mistakes and distractions to make us an easy target to stop the worship of God (1 Thessalonians 4: 1; Colossians 3: 23–24).

Listen, the way the Saints understand themselves is what they will offer to the Almighty. Everybody else expects a ton of virtuousness from believers, yet what they demand rarely agrees with what is significant to them. So, anybody masquerading as something they are not automatically self-drained joy from their spirit.

However, pretending to be another is exhausting. Without confidence, a soul will never reach its full potential. So, build on your God-given skills by reading and studying the Word. Helping those in need is an excellent place to discover the peace of the ALL-MIGHTY. (Philippians 4: 6-7).

When a supporter is obedient to righteousness, they will attract peaceful conceptualization. Others' points of view do not sidetrack them; they tune into their righteous hearts. To ensure a believer stays on track toward goal accomplishment, verify that one's ambitions ally with God's Word. Christians should clarify their purposes and compare them with their objectives. Then keep Divine's goals visible and on one mind 24/7. Set a target to contribute 30 minutes of exploring online Bible verses and sermons daily, reinforcing faithful intention. Calm, relaxing Gospel music can help the Saints be unflustered and focused.

CHAPTER 5

KNOWING ONESELF IN THE LORD THROUGH HIS WORD

True disciples can be much happier once they understand who they unquestionably are in JESUS CHRIST and learn to be themselves. No matter their denomination, He accepts them all devoted to THE LORD's Scripture. When the Saints dedicate their hearts to THE LORD, they reach upward to Him and are thankful for what He has done for them. Love, submission, and devotion to one another are their prime concerns. If we mistreat others, it shows we need to work on our compassion and healing skills.

Someone said, "All wisdom humans possess comprises the knowledge of the Supreme Being and ourselves." The writer trusts their statement to be correct, since every facet of his spiritual life depends on faith in The WORD of Jehovah. The Saint's moral desirability will guide them. But anxiety affects physical health. So, they try to hide their disquieted emotions for someone's encouragement or approval. Or they cry, conscience-stricken about who they are.

Crying is emotional, and the author is not suggesting that it is the only way to unburden stress from the spirit. So, he cautiously moved to his point. Being teary-eyed is not a sign of weakness. Secular society is attempting to build a world with no sorrow. So, they encourage everybody who cries to wipe away those tears. But the Bible says weeping may endure for a night, but joy comes in the morning; Psalm 30: 5 reminds the faithful of the hope we have in THE LORD'S promises that sorrow and suffering are a part of life but will not last forever.

Teardrops allow the Glorified to express their feelings. See Romans 8: 28. The Scripture shows that in any circumstance. Even those that appear to be difficult are leading to success for the Saints, so we need not be worried about the future.

Besides, righteous secretions wash stressful hormones out of the body. They uniformly help relieve pain and can support disciples in mentality-building. Philippians 1: 6 tells us, "He who began a good work in you will bring it to completion on the day of Jesus Christ." So, set bold objectives and forge ahead toward them. Devoted works keep the Savior's Christocentric rejuvenated. Then stay loyal to your holy convictions and views, no matter what anybody else may expect. Repent mistakes and move onward; everybody makes them Christians inclusive.

Categorically stand watchful, carefully consider what is happening and prepare to contend with it. 1 Peter 5: 8 tells the Saints to be calm-minded and alert. "The unholy opponent, the devil, prowls around as a roaring lion, looking for someone to overwhelm with suffering." The 24th chapter of the Gospel of Matthew says that fake messiahs and counterfeit prophets will show up and do miraculous tricks to fool the chosen people.

Satan and his devils have innumerable bamboozle schemes. The Hebrew phrase for Lucifer delineates him as a lying debater, one who hinders, and a blaming-shifting prosecutor. In Greek, his name means adversary. These are a perfect definition for the Prince of Darkness, who brings evil and temptation to mislead humanity.

And if the Archfiend is unsuccessful at causing God's people to follow his ambiguous lies. He persuades them to abandon their prayer and worship commitment. They lack faith in their purpose, leading to a shift away from morality, which causes their self-esteem to suffer.

Lucifer has hundreds of titles in the Sacred Book, depending on the settings or dispensation. But his most horrifying name is Beelzebub, which means fallen angel. In the study of occultism, he is one of the seven deadly demons of the abyss. Therefore, when righteous disciples give an ear to him, they react to less-than-stellar ideas. He is a great deceiver, the most tumultuous of all names, showing how he changed how people saw their connection to the Atoning Sacrifice for our Sins (1 John 2:2).

For instance, in Revelation 12: 9—THE LORD cast (his malignant intention) the Great Dragon out into the earth with his angels. When God drove him from heaven, evil aimed at corrupting morality. Their mandate is to grieve the human disposition, causing them to act sinfully, whether in an idea or physical deed.

So, deceit is a powerful tendency that works treacherously to hoodwink the devoted. It's hard to spot when the Old Serpent is trying to fool Glorified, since he can push ideas and actions that make them think they are being faithful.

Yet, crucifying human nature reminds supporters of what Jesus did for them on the cross. He calls followers to embrace their wrath and follow Him (Matthew 16: 24). Still, we live as sinners when we give in to the flesh. Therefore, we must watch and pray for the Holy Spirit, for he is more significant in the righteous than in their decaying sinful personality.

The Prince of Darkness is the Father of lies (John 8: 44), in tandem with the Ancient Serpent and the Devil. His mandate is to deceive the entire world, causing humanity to be disloyal to Jehovah.

But the Bogeyman's (Satan) more incredible hypocrisy has been in the Church. To show, when believers wrangle around trifling matters, such as which hymns to intone, scuffles over the carpet dye on the floor, etc. It does not matter to the unsympathetic Archfiend who loves a good argument encompassing any topic. He is rejoicing to stir the fire of nefarious passion and pride. It brings him everlasting happiness when the Saints are unappeasable with each other.

They try to appear agreeable but mask their true feelings. Duplicity causes blindness, irresponsibility, and unhappiness among the Saints. Yet, dispute influences Christians to focus on a negative past and fight for nonproductive future events.

The writer is speaking from experience: the effects of unrest are emotional and cause his mental health, nightmares, and physical pain. But Christ's presence in the heart convicts' sin, forgives, and provides a Spirit-controlled life that pleases God (Psalm 19:13).

Still, the Glorified may sometimes stray from the Gospel truth after salvation. But we never forget that the Authoritative Book clarifies that our deliverance from eternal damnation is unmoving (John 10: 28). However, the Supreme Being has authorized no one to indulge in sinful acts. Be watchful. But faith helps to get us through, lighting the pathway of irreproachability in times of darkness.

The Bible says the Supreme Being wants His exalted people's happiness complete (Ephesians 1: 3). Yet, lacking Christian stability robs the canonization of joy and removes the excitement of faithfulness. The Sacred Spirit works to uncover the truth of the Word of God, not to lead the Glorified away from it.

Therefore, the Bible tells supporters to build each other up as Christians. Ill-intended people aim to disrupt Christianity. In Matthew 7: 16, Christ declared the Saints could recognize false prophets by their fruit; undoubtedly, another deleterious bitter melon is an ambiguous teaching which grieves the Holy Spirit.

Supporting balance with hallowed thoughts brings joy. "So, we should sanctify THE LORD God in our hearts and be ready always to answer everyone who asked them a reason for the hope in us, with meekness and fear." 1 Peter 3: 15. Only the Scripture must stay authoritative for calm spirit and peaceful resolutions.

Belaboring the obvious, Christians should beware of accomplished swindlers. They can build false beliefs in a person's lowest manners, especially selfishness, panic, and instability. We know charlatans for their disdain, greed, and gluttony (Jude 1: 11). Materialism overshadows spiritual, intellectual, and cultural values. Their egotistical desires for wealth or power will expose them.

Pseudapostles' only motive is to increase their acquisitions for selfish carnal achievements. They overestimate their self-importance. Their love of things tells how they are defrauders who concentrate on dominance over people.

They impetuously care less about anybody's feelings or their righteousness. Greed leads followers to love possession of evil doctrines or new gadgets. Obsession with wanting more stuff may spin out of control; it is a misleading dreamland that exhausts anybody. Even amid blessings, the Saints can have recurring fits of despair. But for God's individuals, "It will come to pass, that whosoever shall call on the name of Jehovah, He delivers them." Joel 2: 32.

But "The Holy Writ tells us THE LORD is the Supreme Being, and His people should earnestly seek Him; thirst for Him, as in a parched land with no water to drink." Psalm 63: 1.

Yet, faithless adherents are still chasing the conceptualizations of the fleeting idol of money and fame, here now and gone tomorrow. The false hope of materialism is a mask of the fictitious persona that constantly seeks things to support their happiness.

Falsifiers run from the eternal Supreme Being of the universe, "the same yesterday, today, and forever." Carnal disciples presuppose and hypothesize half-truths or whatever sounds good (Ephesians 4: 14). But misinformation can affect your health and well-being and spread faster than the truth.

As for the Gospel, Emmanuel was not a fashionable missionary who advanced in prominence and suddenly retreated into obscurity. His Word tells disciples what is right with transparent motives. Hebrews 13: 8 helps the Saints look backward and forward to understand JESUS' sincerity these days and that what He speaks to us in the heart is true.

So, the truth shows plain differences in how hypocrisy makes believers react. But deceivers spin their untruthfulness to make people happy for the moment. Primarily, they twist the facts to control people's emotions or lie to protect someone's feelings. But these are kind-hearted mendacity and are no better than the worst of disingenuousness.

Self-honesty leads the Glorified to forgive themselves and maintain their inner love; no matter the status quo, they grow and see life as friends. So, the Gospel truth does not offend when we trust the Author of Life Information (Acts 3: 15); Jesus will do nothing to disgruntle the faithful.

THE SUPREME BEING of THE COSMOS foresees a wrongdoer's conversion to righteousness. Pedagogical holiness follows Sacred Principles and sentiments of the heart, then God's Law.

But repent of any wrong before cognizing any God-fearing research. The word repentance is "transforming an individual's mind." It transcends the small-minded ego to stop sinners from ceasing, rationalizing that they are the Creator, so they can yield to the ONE WHO created them. Their understanding reflects: Scriptural repentance is more than just remorse. We see ourselves positively in plain English instead of succumbing to the same weaknesses.

"I have not come to call the righteous, but transgressors to compunction" (Luke 5: 32). Genuine penance is what THE LORD says in His Word. So, to repent means being persuaded by a unique way of belief, which proves more than barely withdrawing from misconduct. Repentance reiterates God's love and forgiveness. He will wipe away your sin and heal your spirit. Besides, this was the focus of JESUS CHRIST'S mission was to recall us to atonement.

Today, the apostolic obliviousness to sin opposes the will and Friendship of Emmanuel. "But your iniquities have separated you from the Divine Father; your sins have hidden His face from you so that He cannot hear." Isaiah 59: 2. God's passion for His people is to have insight through the Holy Spirit.

So, the Christian plea should be that everybody gets the Breath of the Supreme Being and discovers the power of JESUS in the Word. Ignoring Scripture harms us mentally. So, please welcome no unbelief in your life because of a lack of Biblical research.

Thus, the primary complaint of why the Orthodox do not read the Holy Writ is, "They cannot understand it!" So, before you start each inquiry session, begin by praying and seeking THE LORD to open the spiritual understanding. Below are five reprehensible kryptonite concepts to hinder the Saint's prayer and Christian study life.

1. Objectionable notions: Asking with unacceptable motives (James 4: 3)
2. Unconfessed sin: (James 5: 16)
3. Pride: God opposes the proud (James 4: 6)
4. Doubt: Trust THE LORD without suspicion (James 1: 6)
5. Household conflicts: (1 Peter 3: 7)

Five Helpful Hints To Broaden Biblical Studies To lift The Spirit

1. Get the proper Bible transcription. The agreed-upon reading material by evangelicals is essential to investigate Scripture. The NASB is the most accurate English translation. It is the most used version by the Author.
2. Criticisms have mounted about the New World Translation (NWT) and its depiction of the deity and humility of Jesus. The Saints should stay away from this contestable translation.
3. Pick up helpful research capabilities. Before examining the Text, consider collecting resources to support your investigation of the Holy Writ.
4. Inquiries are invaluable to any study. Generate a list of talking points on the Content at hand. Good cross-questions let the reader better understand the Scripture.
5. After reading the Passage, do a historical and cultural environment report. It can be helpful as a believer entering the Biblical world of Christian perception.
6. And finally, do a dialog examination—precisely, key phrases vital to understanding the Theme.

Not heeding the Prime Mover's work increases one's distance from its advantages. (See Romans 3: 23). The inexperience of holiness, hence, sin, overshadows the Saints in judgment and cuts them off from sound discretion. (Ephesians 4: 18). Unskilled in righteousness leads to a sequence of compromises, working against God's Law in our bodies and supplanting it with our own. Too, self-promoting quenches the Spirit of God (1 Thessalonians 5: 19). When we try to make ourselves greater than THE LORD, we are trying to silence what He is saying.

Second, haughtiness is Christian illiterates that build a barricade between the Saint and the Creator. Nobody can serve "two masters." Jesus highlighted, "We cannot serve two masters." Unfaithfulness brings changes in righteousness that cause behavioral distress.

Therefore, because Jehovah is Holy, He cannot overlook, excuse, or condone unintelligence towards Scripture as though it does not matter (2 Timothy 2: 15). For instance, the Church of Ephesus was significant in the first century. Yet, the Apostle Paul warned them wildly surrounding the lack of Biblical knowledge. "Being darkened in understanding will exclude from the life of the Supreme Being." (Ephesians 4: 18).

Further, ignorance of the Scripture results in moving away from the Gospel. Tricked by stupidity, one convinces themselves they do not need the wisdom of JESUS. Yet, once anybody creates doubtful disunion thoughts relevant to the Faithful Witness, they can see no value in Christian Education. So, they have no choice but to put their hope in materialism, the order that eats them from the inside outward. But the primary danger of immoderation advances to excessive and lacking restraint. Intemperance manifests in disheartened spirits, and out-of-control behavior shows wickedness.

But the Holy Writ recounts the origin of sin, death, war, subjugation, persecution, and crucifixion. Its narratives tell of struggles and how to overcome them. The Word tells us the rewards of good humor and how to build on undisputed love. So, when the spirit is suffering or shattered, seek God; hence, we can find refuge and strength in Him. The Authoritative Book follows a simple storyline: the Father establishing His kingdom at the creation of nature. And how from the foundation of the world, THE LORD wanted someone to fellowship with, so He created humankind.

Further, The New Testament details how people of The Righteous go directly into the presence of the All-Mighty after death (Luke 23: 43; 2 Corinthians 5: 8; Philippians 1: 23). Christian Doctrine teaches the reader that JESUS CHRIST is not only the Son of God but gave His Life as a sacrifice for humanity's sins. Hence, this alone is a spirit lifter. In doing so, He ensured everlasting continuance for anyone who trusted Him. (John 3: 16–18; Romans 10: 9). Only those with a pure heart will achieve everlasting life, and the only way to know righteousness in the eyes of the Almighty is through trust in the Gospel.

The Son of the Almighty atoned for mortal's sins, so He commands humankind everywhere to repent (Acts 17: 30). Carnal followers mistakenly think repentance is only feeling sorrow and expecting success. Evaluate for yourself to see if this idea helps you. First, realize no individuals are pure but Jehovah. So, "I am a perfect person" is an individual belief, so let this concept go if it does not work for you. Second, no one can know them unless they understand themselves in THE LORD. Besides, perfectionists trap themselves in the past, worried about a future outcome.

> *Romans 3: 10-20 tells us: "No human is righteous, no, not any; There is none who understands; There is none who seeks after God. Everybody has turned aside; They have together become unprofitable; none does good, no, not a single person."*

Max Lucado said well: The Bible's central theme is salvation through faith in Christ. So, a hunger for the Messiah, THE LORD over sin, is not around one's emotions or conduct modification. The Word communicates to Christians how to commit to God.

The Holy Writ allows the sinner another chance to trust the Author of Redemption, Passion, and Forgiveness, then adhere to His righteousness. Through the grace of the Alpha and Omega, the SAVIOR, humans can repent and spiritually grow and thrive. No other name under Heaven (except JESUS) people can have salvation (Acts: 4: 12).

CHAPTER 6

CHRIST, THE AUTHOR OF ALL THINGS

The Creator (Jesus) is "The Author of Salvation (Hebrew 2: 10), Who is the architect of the beginning of life and matter (John chapter 1: 1-3)." Unlike most individuals, He is the Alpha and Omega in the narrative of God's authorship. So, He determines responsibility for what He has created. Thus, He has robust personal accountability for His masterwork and does not depend on others. Cause and effect are the thousand realizations that THE LORD plays a part in every condition of humanity's experience. Romans 2: 1-29.

Jehovah's Word is the Body, Soul, and Paraclete of Jesus, the Firstborn, over All His achievement (Colossians 1: 15, John 1: 1-3). Since His conception by the Sacred Spirit in the womb of the Virgin Mary (Luke 1: 26-38), skeptics have questioned His Supremacy.

Regardless, the Bible tells us the relationship between what He SPOKE, the Wisdom of God, or events that caused what He UTTERED. Immanuel is the Last Adam having the same accomplished powers as the Supreme Being. Yet, He is the Atoning Sacrifice for humans' Sins; thus, the Father imbued Him with Absolutely Divinity within the Holy Triad.

The Holy Trinity, comprising the Divine Being, Son, and Hallowed Spirit, possesses the highest righteousness. And then, They UNITE in the long-standing edict of creation that determines the fate of His people. For example, Genesis 1: 1, "In the beginning, the Deity created the heavens and the earth." THE LORD'S Words brought tangible and intangible conceptualizations into existence.

But, in GENESIS 1: 26 KJV, When THE LORD declared, "*Let Us Form Man In Our Image*," this shows humanity did not emerge from an alternative lesser formation of a creature. The Supreme Being plurality terminology also suggests the unity of Father, Son, and Holy Spirit as three persons in one Godhead.

God asked for His Son's and Holy Spirit's help in human creation (Genesis 1:26). No mention of cherubs creating in the Bible. God's Words created life forms and universes: "Let Us Make." So, we have a clue of the Triumvirate with the plural title Elohim in "Multiplicity but ONE."

The Trinity is a doctrine to help us understand One God as three coequal, coeternal, and Indistinguishable Divine Persons. Pagans and most Christians find it hard to comprehend Trinitarianism.

Despite this, an effortless way to understand the Trinity is: The Father is accountable for creation. Jesus Christ brings this to life, and the Holy Spirit is the bridge between them and the ultimate revelation of Jehovah and the Son.

However, learning the role of the Head of the Church (Ephesians 1: 22; 4: 15; 5: 23) as the Creator is the elegance of expressing God. Valuing God's creation shows reverence.

Sharing the Gospel shows we do not just execute salvation duties for it—but we undertake to make Christianity our vocation. Righteous behavior results in Godly influence. To show forth the power of Yahweh through witnessing is a fantastic way to highlight your love for righteousness.

But after God created the human species, He instilled their free will. Yet, they acted on their freedom to transgress against the Heavenly Father's Law. So, Jesus comes to earth to destroy the devil's work and unshackles people held in fear of death. He who does what is sinful is from the devil because he has sinned from the beginning (1 John 3: 8). Still, (Jesus), the Head of the Church, sacrificed his life for humanity.

So, BEYOND ANY DOUBT, THE MASTER of THE UNIVERSE is THE LAST ADAM (1 Corinthians 15: 45), THE PRINCE OF PEACE, THE SUPREME BEING, and THE FOUNDING PRIME MOVER of human restoration. The Lamb Without Blemish (Jesus) (1 Peter 1: 19) declared that He is the way, the truth, and the life and that no individual comes to the ALMIGHTY LORD except through Him (John 14: 6). God plans to bring humans back to their original holy state. Jehovah restores through humans' acceptance of His Heir, JESUS THE NAZARENE.

For example, an official asked in Mark 2: 7 after Jesus forgave a person's sins. "Why does this man speak in the fashion of wrongdoing amnesty? Only The Most-High can excuse immoral acts; He is blaspheming!" These men told the truth, unknowingly calling attention to their assessment of the Prince of Peace's power to forgive sins. But Jehovah was overlooking personal, unethical behavior through the Human Form of the Righteous Branch (Jeremiah 23: 5) as the Redeemer!

Perfect intent, impartiality, and administration in 1 Peter 2: 6 is God's moral concept. So, the forgiveness of transgression is one of the principal parts of justification originated by THE ALL-MIGHTY. It starts with an open admission, where one humbly acknowledges their offenses before THE LORD and concedes to their missteps. Making amends for violations of His Sacred Law is crucial.

The Psalmist reads: "THE LORD is kind and merciful...He pardons every single one of your iniquities; He heals without exception your ills...Not according to our sins does He react to us" (Psalm 103). Yet, this does not mean God closes His eyes or turns His back when humans sin. Understanding Jehovah's righteous nature is crucial in comprehending His approach to wrongdoings.

Salvation begins the Messiah's grace toward humankind, and He causes everything seen and unseen (John 1: 1-3). THE MASTER of THE UNIVERSE made transgression liberation possible by dying on the cross for humanity's wrongdoing. The contribution of liberty from misdoings of man's freedom is from THE LORD, Jesus. God promises to cleanse us from all unrighteousness if we confess our sins in 1 John 1:9.

So, the embodiment of the Creator's purpose for coming to the planet was to bring a message of love and liberation to humanity. And reveal His Righteous Character. Scripture teaches: "In Yahweh, the totality of the fullness of the Deity lives in bodily form" (Colossians 2: 9).

Apostle Paul explains in the Scripture above that the Almighty is always three Persons—the Father, Son, and Holy Spirit—with no end. JESUS' conception by the Breath of the King of kings in the womb of the Virgin Mary (Luke 1: 26-38) is the real identity of Jehovah's infallible living soul embodiment. And His death, burial, and resurrection are the fundamental act of deliverance to humankind.

So, the Author of Life has unlimited authority and can do whatever (Psalm 115: 3). He is the Begetter Who begot the Son through the Holy Spirit, and then He creates altogether through Him. Jesus is the Primary Cause of salvation, as in 2 Corinthians 5: 17.

"Hence, if anybody is in the Faithful Witness, he is a unique creation. The Apostle Paul is straightforward; individuals who belong to the Lamb Without Blemish have become different. He proclaims familiar things have passed away. Their traditional body is gone, and an extraordinary life has begun; "behold, the new has come."

THE LORD'S field of perception of humankind in the Redeemer is righteous. He views the Glorified instantaneously and justifies Christians through Christ's righteousness. So, the Creator does not condescendingly look at our misdeeds (Romans 8: 1). Jesus has freed us from our guilt. So, the Supreme Being forgives us of our sins and restores our relationship with the Father. (See I John 3: 8–10).

Instead, THE LORD sees His disciples clothed in the Deity's grace. Specifically, JESUS' foundational sacrificial death transformed the believer from the curse of sin (Mark 10: 45). But His demise had a far-reaching implementation on humankind since He sacrificed His Life in their place. Again, such people who receive salvation through Him are now new creatures. Saved Christians' standing has changed from being trivial to having godly morality.

The Bible tells the humans of The Man from Glory's involvement in creation, Who is Heaven's Almighty, Who said: "Let us make humankind in our image" (Genesis 1: 26). He and Jehovah are the same (John 10:30), the Mediator of the New Covenant (Hebrew 9: 15), The Heavenly Father, and the Transmitter, and Architect of salvation. The Supreme Being (Christ) is the Designer and Builder (Hebrews 11: 10), demonstrating His standing as the Creator of everything visible and invisible.

If the Bible has grammatical human misquotes, it is not about whether Jesus is THE LORD. He claimed to be Jehovah in the Gospel of John. The Gospels show no oversights by THE SON. So, we could accept He made no misstatements. Hence, His assertion excludes any prospect of inaccuracy in achieving His Deity's goal with the Father. THE LORD'S uprightness includes each of His Commandments and goes beyond to have the Covenant of His people. Thus, the virtuousness of Yahweh Is in Immanuel (and what He Is in the spirit of Truth).

To recapitulate, the Infinite Divine initially spoke, created bare land, and gathered the waters from the terrain, calling it dry ground. It was a formal way of Jehovah saying: The Godhead is ONE God in Three Persons: Father, Son, and Holy Spirit.

As the Originator spoke, the earth's surface responded positively. Rather than relying on outdated superstitions, this is where humanity's practical efforts begin. God's Commandment confirms eternal life and presence through Jesus Christ.

In John 8: 42, the Author of Salvation knew that the Almighty had put everything under His power. And that he emerged from the Father and someday He will return to Him. His statement, "I come from God," is a most remarkable word, not describing a fellowship of nearness to the Alpha-and-Omega, but an essential one.

THE LORS'S undertone suggestion, "He has His origins in the Godhead," is a literal understanding: He is The Mediator of the New Covenant. The Good Shepherd left the primary mystery of Being Equal with JEHOVAH. He did not emerge from standing in the Suprema's presence Being or having togetherness with the King of Heaven as an angel.

Jesus Christ was the Spoken Word, to cause the ground's dust to produce the anatomy in a procedure Yahweh breathes life into man's soul. Yet, the writer believes The Godhead had a more significant meaning for the Trinity. To show humankind that exceptional individuals should modestly respect those under their leadership.

CHAPTER 7

THE GENUINENESS OF JESUS

Pure Holiness required Immanuel to be the Supreme Being and human because homo sapiens cannot save themselves. But to pass the definitive test of the Godman, the Ruler of God's Creation had to withstand the suffering for humanity's sins. Jesus faced temptation and physical vulnerability. He ate proper food and died as we do.

God's Son is The Author of Salvation, Who faced the same testing humanity does. The writer of Hebrew tells the readers: "We do not have a high priest unable to sympathize with our weaknesses." Hebrews 4: 15. His compassions mean He cares relevant to us. But even though He lived as a human, He did not commit immoral acts against His Divine Law.

Yes, Jesus died, but unlike humankind's death, THE LORD'S Holy Spirit resurrected Him with all power on the third day by the Breath of the Almighty (John 20: 22). So, the empty tomb is the most decisive proof the Head of the Church sprang from a lifeless body. Christianity's growth is likewise evidence of the authenticity of Christ's Deity. His inner disciples talked with Him alive after He rose from the grave. They were eyewitnesses of His resurrection. Though more than that, five hundred followers saw Him at one time, the Apostle Paul wrote in (1 Corinthians 15: 6).

So, only the Author and Perfecter of our Faith (Who is the King of the Ages, Revelation 15: 3)) was acceptable as a perfect sacrifice for humankind's sin to Jehovah. Christ offered His Body as a peace offering to the Lord to fulfill a special vow for humanity's sins.

Therefore, the Father and the Son, and the Holy Spirit are coequal in sanctification. However, Jesus became the Hope of Glory for reconciliation between humanity and God. (Romans 5: 5-6).

Nobody except Immanuel could ever reach the faultless hallmark of morality. Still, most humanity follows pagan superstitions, searching for a more profound moral truth. But that is impossible and results in a rebellious, sinful nature.

That being so, apart from Christ, humanity has no other name under heaven given to people by which they can save themselves." Acts 4: 12. Jesus is the only way to redemption for billions of reasons. But the fundamental cause is that God favored him as the Faithful Witness. The Bible says, "As you come to Him, a living stone rejected by men, yet the Supreme Being chose Him to be the Precious Savior" (1 Peter 2: 4).

So, without faith in Emmanuel's death, burial, and resurrection; hence, redemption would be merely a fictitious delusion, pretending to be Holy. To the restoration of the Firstborn From the Dead (Jesus), a righteous believer's faith is in the experience of HIS SACRED INTEGRITY. And Christians trust His identity as the sinless SAVIOR, the Supreme Being, Who came to earth in Human Form. Besides the above, we can know Christ's authenticity by experiencing True Conviction in the Holy Spirit.

The Greek word elencho means to convince someone with facts or reality until they accept their misdeeds, which is where the phrase convict comes from. Specifically, when Isaiah stood in the presence of God, he was at once overwhelmed by his unholiness: "Woe to me, I am ruined" (Isaiah 6: 5)! So, until we come to terms with our wrongdoings, the Holy Spirit acts as a pursuing criminal lawyer who uncovers evil and sways us; we need to repent.

> *Once more, Colossians 2:9 tells readers, "For in THE FIRSTBORN OVER every Creation dwells the fullness of The Godhead bodily. John 10: 28-30 - I give them eternal life, and they can never perish, nor shall any man pluck them from my hand."*

Deceptive accounts can influence wrong interpretations. Without exception, we must share The Hope of Glory, as His disciples did. They had a protracted reality relevant to (Christ) the Head of the Church (Ephesian1: twenty-two; 4: 15; 5: 23).

The writer also knows God's Son is true because he had an intimate experience with the Lord of Glory, the Messiah. But anyone can have a personal relationship with the Almighty; (Jesus Christ). He is no respecter of persons, Deuteronomy 10: 17 Therefore, He contributes to his righteousness by witnessing the Good News of Holiness.

Still, they must accept the gift of redemption and include the Blessed and only Ruler daily. Because, while doing our faith walk, sin could be a constant battle. Thus, we must call out to the All-Mighty for support. Then, believe in His promises, and Jehovah will transform your life.

The Savior helps Bishop Bingham, and (he) enthusiastically tells others of his release from sin. Christ's undisputed grace provides justice to anybody who sincerely seeks his help; see 1 Peter 1: 17. The wordsmith has shared his salvation testimony at church with small groups, family, friends, and strangers. He has likewise shared his virtuous affirmation in books, blogs, and journals. Doctor Bingham lets everybody he meets know that Jesus is authentic in his soul and could be in theirs.

Theists and hundreds of historians note the reputable evidence of Immanuel's miracles. The Apostles were happy with a powerful and awe-inspiring hope in the wake of Jesus Christ's death and resurrection. Then, they worship Him as the Father Jehovah after His Reappearance following a three-day loss of life.

Ancient texts, artifacts, and eyewitness accounts prove Jesus existed. Yet, Agnostics repeatedly state that inaccessible to explain the resurrection of Jesus. But that is not correct. Peter and John ran to the tomb, looked inside, and saw it was empty.

Further, worldly and theological scholars accept the historical existence of Christ. Secular sources attest to the Lamb of God's miracles, crucifixion, and resurrection. So, ancient data shows that the Son of the King of Kings lived.

For instance, in the Gospel of Luke, his geographical and cultural statements and landmarks have proven correct. The archaeologists show the New Testament is authentic, and (Jesus) the Lion of the Tribe of Judah is the Main Individual.

There is, too, a wealth of conclusive testimony of Immanuel that substantiates the Biblical account of His resurrection. The prosecution of the Apostles and the surge of Jewish and non-Jewish converts to Christianity enabled the proliferation of the faith. Their conversion is evidence that THE FIRSTBORN OVER ALL CREATION is the God-Man.

So, John composed two of his three short Letters to end doubtful erroneous theories encompassing THE LORD'S Deity. He asserted that individuals who physically acknowledge the Great High Priest belong to the Supreme Being. Those who don't recognize the Church's Head in physical form are not part of God (1 John 4: 2-3). John began his Letter by specifying that he heard, saw, and touched with his hands (Jesus) the "Word of Life, which was with the Father in the beginning." Someone did not create Jesus, but He is the Co-Creator of the Triad.

"The Father and I are One" (John 10:30); "He who sees Me sees the One who sent Me" (John 12:45); and "He who has seen Me has seen the Father" (John 14:9-10).

Further proof of Christ, the King Eternal, is His unique attributes. The Son showed the qualities of the Almighty altogether. Despite the lack of belief in the Lamb of Jehovah by specific individuals of His time, He still manifested His Divine powers as a Human Being Incarnated. The writer encourages the Saints to stop limiting God by their disbelief of what He can do in their lives. Give Him your faith and watch Him collaborate with you. THE LORD cannot bless what you do not believe. (Deuteronomy. 28: 8).

Matthew 13: 58, "And He did not do many miracles there because of their unbelief. Christ had all Divine Qualities, including All-Knowingness, Everywhere Present, and All-Powerful. His glory shone through his grace and integrity (John 1:14).

Jesus Christ, being The Firstborn of the Dead from Heaven, is constantly alive in the past, the present, and the future (Hebrews 13: 8). "JESUS CHRIST is the same yesterday, today, and eternal." In Isaiah 40: 8, the Bible states, "The grass withers, the flower fades, but the Word of our God will stand forever."

In the Savior's lifetime, they called the Offspring of Joseph (Luke 4: 22; John 1: 45, 6: 42), the Nazareth (Acts 10: 38), or the Nazarene (Mark 1: 24; Luke 24: 19). After his death, they hailed Him Holy and True. Christ is a Name inferred from the Greek Word Christos, which translates to the Hebrew term Messiah, meaning "the Blessed One."

His titles prove that JESUS' disciples understood him as the Anointed Heir of King David. Yet, an unspecified number of Jews still await THE LORD to restore His chosen individuals to their kingdom. They believe in "a Savior" who can usher in an age of righteousness and peace and redeem the Jewish people in exile. But the Son of God has consistently fulfilled every redemptive assignment.

However, The New Testament Covenant proclaims The Author of Salvation as the Redeemer in Matthew 1:16. They pointed to His coming to the Pentateuch or the Five Books of Moses. But the "NAME" "Christ" describes Jesus as the Anointed One in the New Testament.

Subsequently, the New Testament ratified Jesus as the Messiah of Nazareth. The Prophets declare He will be a Hebrew Man (Isaiah 9: 6) delivered in Bethlehem (Micah 5: 2) of a virgin (Isaiah 7: 14), a Prophet interchangeable to Moses (Deuteronomy 18: 18).

A note, Immanuel is the Priest in the order of Melchizedek (Psalm 110: 4), a King (Isaiah 11: 1–4), and the Son of David (Matthew 22: 42) who suffered before coming into His Majesty (Isaiah 53). The Creator of Life satisfied each of these Divine conditions. We should never look for a savior elsewhere than in Jesus; we have Him in the Word of God (John 5:39).

CHAPTER 8

JESUS' DEATH HAD REDEMPTIVE PURPOSES

Humanity's vindication, peace of mind, and atonement are benefits of Christ's harsh treatment. But the religious hypocrites of Jesus' day did not allow the realism of Holiness to take root in their hearts. These Jewish teachers and leaders of His time could not acknowledge the deity of Christ's acceptable Glorious purpose. Instead, they made Him suffer and crucified Him. His death atoned for humanity and completed righteousness.

Too, Jesus' death on the cursed tree opened a path to salvation and empowered everybody to have a positive relationship with Him. His death paid the penalty for our sins (1 Corinthians 15: 3; 2 Corinthians 5: 21), for which we deserve eternal separation from God because of the first parent's sin (Romans 6: 23). However, He is the Alpha and Omega; hence, we can live forever when we believe in Him (Revelation 1: 8; 22: 13-14). But He will not clear the guilt, visiting the iniquity of the fathers on the children to the third and the fourth generations.'

THE LORD'S death is the most significant cause of the cross as a symbol of atonement. Jesus recompensed human sins at Calvary by conquering the devil and shaping Christianity. With His death on the cross, Jesus cancels the record of debt that stood against humanity.

With this, "He withdrew the charge of humanity's legal indebtedness, which stood against humans and condemned them; in doing so, He has taken control of condemnation away, nailing our trespasses to the cross." (Colossians 2: 14).

Again, it was symbolic that Jesus died on the cursed tree so we would not have to (Galatians 3: 13). Humankind must ask for forgiveness of sins; this will remind them of the price Christ paid for their redemption. Inarguably, His graceful Love is why God gave His Son for sinners. We can discover God's riches through grace as we look to the cross for our lives. He has given us an unrestricted gift. Grace is THE LORD'S unwarranted love and favor.

Therefore, Jesus, the Son of God, death has made Him The Author of Life for humans who repent. Being the Creator of all existence, He can sympathize and relate to His people on a human level, as He took on a flawed form to redeem the corrupted bodies of humanity. Hence, He sees humankind as individuals of value. Unequivocally, the writer implores everybody to give the Heir of All Things (Hebrew 1: 2) a chance.

It was significant to note that Immanuel's parting from life was not standard but of humanity's unrighteousness. In His view, every human in themselves is unrighteous despite their continuing attempts to be otherwise. The first parents' disobedience led to self-righteousness, which displeased God.

Still, God justifies humans (declared them right) with Him on behalf of Jesus, THE FIRSTBORN OVER ALL Creation's sacrificial death. Isaiah 7: 14. (Jesus) The Head of the Church, His last exit from life, was significant because His departure covered our grievous fault; it redeemed transgression. Assuredly, anybody who trusts in THE LORD JESUS CHRIST for their salvation is dead to sin and alive to God's grace.

The Hope of Glory died to bring us to God (1 Thessalonians 5:10). Thus, in righteous conceptualization, The Prince of Peace gave His

Life to everybody who repents. Now equally, they may continue simultaneously with Him, whether awake or asleep (John 15: 13). Still, we must atone for or acknowledge our sins, stray from them, and shift toward a life of Holy conformity.

Lacking softheartedness or understanding of Biblical repentance through Christ's death contradicts one's beliefs. Precisely, most individuals sense a need to apologize when caught not doing right.

However, a believer's genuine remorse is not sorrow or fearing punishment; that is not true repentance. That is stubbornness when Christians refuse to look to the cross for forgiveness when they know they are wrong. These obstinate folks are narcissists who see fault in everyone but themselves. They are primarily liars who claim to be sorry when they are not.

JESUS is the embodiment of truth. He is the personification of integrity. And the reference position for calculating outright consecrated sincerity. He was born to fulfill Old Testament promises and prophecies. So, we can only realize genuine repentance when we appeal through His death, burial, and resurrection.

Therefore, moral uprightness and integrity can break hatred, bias, and mistrust. The death of Christ on the cross, as described in Hebrews 9:15, gives a greater purpose to our relationship with God. Thus, His mortality allows us to experience God's grace in the face of his wrath.

The Blessed and Only Ruler's death on the crucifix intersects with the Supreme Being's love and justice. And everyone who belongs to honesty listens to the Alpha and Omega Voice. With the purpose that humankind would escape the curse of the Law.

The terminology "dead to sin" comes from Romans 6: 11. The cross of Jesus is an indisputable truth. And so, a heartfelt act of reparation for those who accept and move because Christ wiped away our sins with his crucifixion. Thus, we can resist evil and reject everything God hates. Or, at least, embrace what he adores.

THE LORD'S death on the tree left the perfect righteousness of the Highest Priesthood (Hebrew 4: 14) alive in believers' hearts. Jesus' crucifixion shows we are one with His in His suffering and work together for the Good Works of the Father. "For we are His craft-workers, created in Christ Jesus unto greatness." So, the cross must be central to our Christian faith. Thus, let us stop looking past it to share an empty tomb.

The Scripture distinction clarifies that to be "paralyzed to transgression" is to be "conscious of The Deity in Christ JESUS." Therefore, "count yourselves lifeless to transgression but alive to Jehovah to The Lamb Without Blemish." Those who have enlightened themselves about the cross and believe in sin do not control them. Instead, they surrender themselves to God to follow His purposes. So, the cross that symbolizes Jesus' death was also a path to His and our resurrection to eternal life.

Jesus' death for the sins of others differs from a regular passing. His disciples went astray shortly after the soldiers crucified Him, proving He was dead. They murdered THE LORD for no provocation of wrongdoings.

But the Scripture also points out that they worshiped Him as the Living God after His resurrection! We should celebrate the Man from Heaven's sacrifice with worship and joy. His ascension signifies the end of His earthly work and the beginning of our eternal life with Him in Glory (John 14: 3-10).

Now, by grace and mercy, we should recognize how the death of ONE Godman could achieve so much incontestably. JESUS' death proves that an individual can stay devoted to the Heavenly Father through the most trying tests. Even when challenged with the sharpest trials (Hebrews 4: 15), repentance is always in order. God wants us to be modest enough to confess when we are dishonest.

There is no best time to confess one's sins; any time is good. But especially when we hear the preaching of Jesus, the Author of Salvation Word. He told us that His sheep understand His sovereign calling. And that the world (the unsaved) cannot receive His Holy Spirit. Therefore, they cannot hear His Voice the same as the righteous believer (John 10; 14: 17). He is the Firstborn From the Dead Who died for "the forgiveness of humanity's transgressions. Sin is the transgression of God's Law (1 John 3: 4), and "the soul who sins shall perish."

But the individual who does not practice sin will endure after death. Sadly, the one who consistently exercises sin without remorse does not have the DNA of the Author of Salvation. Thus, amnesty is impossible for those who practice iniquity. Those who practice righteousness believe that they will live perpetually. Eternal life is the significant foundation of the death of Christ. So, the significance of the cross is not the architect or construction, but it is the symbol of Jesus' death, reminding humankind they can be free of sin.

When a believer shows remorse, it signifies the purging of sin and wrongdoings, or departing from them, when they appeal to THE LORD for absolution. JESUS died in humankind's place for their sins. Christ's sacrificial death removed the anger of the Father that humanity justly deserved. Indisputably, human penance goes even further than being sorrowful for wrongdoings. Doctor Bingham will speak more, touching on repentance in another chapter.

Jesus, the Leader of the Church, gave up His Life to appease God's wrath. The Father took the disgrace of homo sapiens' trespass away from them and placed it on The Hope of Glory, Who satisfied humankind's guilt by His loss of life.

Again, JESUS takes away and expiates our sins. Thus, in John 1:29, John the Baptist calls JESUS: "the Lamb of God who removes the sins of the world." Likewise, Isaiah 53: 6 tells us, "THE LORD has caused the iniquity of humanity to fall on Him," Hebrews 9: 26 says,

"The Author of Salvation put away humanity's fall from grace; by the sacrifice of Himself." Atoning and securing remission of sins for us and reconciliation to God. "Without the shedding of blood, absolutely no forgiveness of sins" (Hebrew 9: 22; Leviticus 17: 11).

CHAPTER 9

PURPOSE OF THE FATHER, SON, AND HOLY SPIRIT

Doctor Bingham will start with the Holy Spirit and work backward. The Spirit of Truth imparts Godly benefits. He is the Divine Paraclete Who manifests Himself through the Spiritual gifts of wisdom, knowledge, faith, and Holiness.

Saints should be enthusiastic about collaboration to develop the Fruits of the Comforter.

Christianity Unity instructs the Glorified to increase their power in their most minor and arduous efforts. Unconditionally, the Exalted must continue to embrace human differences. Embracing racial and ethnic inclusion shows that everyone has a part to play in the congregation's commonwealth. Serving in unity can be challenging, but with God's guidance, the returns are great, and each parishioner can thrive in their faith.

The Saints emerge as a better version of Christlike when they are proficient in the benefits of the Supernatural Being. Ephesians 4: 14-16 outlines the Apostle Paul's vision for the growth and unity of the local Church, emphasizing the importance of diversity. But the most relevant passage on spiritual abilities is in Galatians 5: 22-23. Christians learn how to be more righteous with the help of the Holy Spirit through Education about the fruits of the Spirit.

The Divine Providence is the disciples' Sacred Companion (John 14: 26). He frees from hardship, reinvigorates, and reaffirms the believer's righteousness (Titus 3: 5). Thus, the Triad live together as One as the Christian believers should do so. The Pure Spirit seals Christians until redemption, showing the Spirit of Truth is irreversible.

God, Jesus, is the Paraclete Who preserves and maintains the restoration of the ones they indwell (Ephesians 1: 13; 4: 30). The Holy Spirit is the Intercessor, and its vital role is to aid those who worship in prayer (Jude 1:20). Assist them in praying in line with The Father's wishes (Romans 8:26–27).

God's Breath of Holiness is neither an "attractiveness" nor an "impulse." He is the Paraclete, the Same as The Almighty and the Alpha and Omega. The Spirit is The Breath of God's purpose, allowing Christians to live humble lives. The Prime Mover is the Third Person of the Righteous Triad.

Jehovah's Holy Spirit's power, positional number, does not limit His sovereignty. His Triunity Relationship with the deity proves He is the Living Entity, yet still the Beginning and End. In knowing so, we should not call Him an allurement heard in the star wars movie: The Rise of Skywalker, quoting the phrase ("THE FORCE BE WITH YOU").

For instance, All Three Deities have a moral purpose woven into the fellowship for humanity. God the Father causes material elements. He sent JESUS to die on the cross for humanity's sins, and the Paraclete's role is to guide the believers into the truth (John 16: 13). The Triumvirate, in unison, makes up the Trichotomy Love Relationship as the exclusive Supreme Being.

But under no circumstances is Trinitarianism a belief in triplex pagan symbols. Jehovah is the Sole Blessed Ruler, and Christians must never stray from the Three in One Deity conceptualization. The Almighty is a Holy Individual in the operational Spirit of the Sanctified Trilogy as the single Savior. Still, Tri-Unitarianism confuses Saints and nonbelievers. By portraying the Supreme Being as three symbols of power on a throne, they diminished His grandeur and restricted Jesus' Atoning Sacrifice.

The human mind is finite and cannot unravel overall the scope and intensity of the Almighty's Individuality (John 4: 24). The Almighty Is not "just any spirit;" HE Is "THE SPIRIT." SPIRIT Is HIS INHERENT QUALITIES- HE is not a physical being. Christians accept the Trinity by faith and credit God's grace, even though they cannot understand it.

Thus, to be THREE IN ONE is possible. Deuteronomy chapter 29: 29 states that the Lord our Father holds undisclosed qualities. Whereas we, along with our children, adhere to the visible elements of this Law forever.

The Supreme Being is TRIUNE INDIVIDUALS: the Father, the Son, and the Holy Spirit. Again, He is not a trio fetish. When Christians say THE King of kings is the Second Person of the Trinity, we do not mean He is a separate Individual or a triple-headed man sitting on a throne. That would be abnormal! By "PERSON," we imply a real being who can think, comprehend, and choose.

For instance, when believers pray, the LIVING SOULS of the REDEEMER work together. We implore the Father, and He answers. The Son helps us as we intercede. The Spirit lives inside Christians, giving them the strength to know what to supplicate. He, too, explains the essential foundation of life's motive (Jeremiah 1: 5). Still on the doorstep of Holiness, countless things apply to the Author of Life that humankind cannot explain. Specifically, the trilogy is one subject because God Is more consequential than humans' thoughts (see Deuteronomy 29: 29).

Unlike humanity, the LORD is " SINGULAR," a Perfectly Unique Being. In a conceptual sense, when attempting to comprehend the

Triune. We may apprehend the usefulness of the Triad's Holiness as adherents of Christianity. Physical limitations prevent us from understanding the Triumvirate Unity of grace and mercy until the LORD frees our souls.

Too, we cannot grapple with our narrow terrestrial thinking and force it onto God. In comparison, we should believe in the Triune Godfather, Son, and Holy Spirit—as the Divine power and allow trust and righteousness to guide a sinful world.

> *Again, when Christians speak of the Almighty, they mean Jehovah. Both the Son and the Almighty Creator are the Alpha and Omega, and Jesus' Breath is the Holy Spirit.*

According to Christian theology, the Trinity confirms the existence of God, the Son, and the Holy Spirit as a single entity. The Plurality of Beings and Unity of Essence. What is the basis for Christians to accept this Doctrine? Three reasons:

- It is a genuine Biblical belief; Matthew 3: 16, Matthew 12: 28, Matthew 28: 19, Luke 3: 22, John 14: 26, John 15: 26, Acts 1: 4, and more.
- Prophets of the Old Testament (see Isaiah 48: 16) show God in Threesome Personage, Genesis 1: 26, Genesis 3: 22, Genesis 11: 7, Isaiah 6: 8, Colossians 1: 15-17, and more.
- So, the Holy Book is monotheistic. The Manuscripts tell us that THE TRIUNE Presences of Jehovah and the Triad Individuals are the same but independent power. EPHESIANS 4: 6 shows the reader "ONE Supreme Being AND THE LORD of HOSTS and YHWH RULER over EVERYBODY, Who Is OVER EVERYTHING." The Bible shares no alternative interpretation that makes sense for the Trinity.

The Divine Being indivisibly reconciles in Three Entities: Yahweh, Jesus of Nazareth, and the Holy Spirit. These Threesomes are the "SOURCE" of Human Salvation.

THE FATHER, SON, and THE PARACLETE are of equal stature, eternal, possessing the same temperament and character, and worthy of equal reverence. Study Matthew 3: 16, 17; Matthew 28: 19-20; Mark 12: 29; John 1: 14; Acts 5: 3, 4, and 2 Corinthians 13: 14.

Anew, the writers of the Authoritative Book, explain the Trinity in Jewish Law and the Gospel. The Pentateuch and Prophets teach it by ramification, but the New Covenant is transparent, without vagueness or ambiguity. An instance, the Bible comprises various accounts reacting to the unification of the Creator. Deuteronomy 6: 4 states, "THE LORD IS RIGHTEOUS INDEPENDENT." 1 Corinthians 8: 4 reads that " Jehovah is Singular." 1 Timothy 2: 5 asserts that "He is undivided." Every adherent of the Bible fervently proclaims this truth.

So, belief in the Trinity is profoundly significant for building holistic righteousness. Christian communion with the Creator of Life (Acts 3:15) fosters a greater comprehension that the Believers are the Tri-Union offspring. He is Our Triad-Personal Savior! They are the Divine standard for the Glorified reconciliation: the Father through the Son and in the Holy Spirit (Ephesians 2: 18). But Ephesians 2: 11–22 points out how we, in JESUS CHRIST, belonged to the part of a single-family of righteousness.

CHAPTER 10

UNDERSTANDING THE HUMAN NATURE

Compared to the TRIAD FATHER, who is the personification of intellectual morality. Humans comprise three parts that incline them to sin. So, for most humans, believing in God is easy, but our core values and beliefs do not suddenly disappear when someone becomes a Christian. The individual's makeup disagrees with Holiness to do the opposite of what THE LORD expects. So, in this chapter, when we speak of the flesh, we refer to human nature.

The Letter of Paul to the Galatians warns them. "Now the works of one's individuality are clear: sexual immorality, impurity, sensuality, idolatry, sorcery, enmity, strife, jealousy, fits of anger, rivalries, dissensions, divisions, envy, drunkenness, orgies, and like these. As I warned you before, I warn you that those who do such dishonorableness will not inherit the kingdom of God." Galatians 5:19-21.

But where did the immoral human character originate? Romans 5: 12. The first father's sin is the "Original Immoral act" or the "Unethical behavior of Adam," which comes down to all of humanity. Adam's disobedience caused all men to fall short of the Father's moral standard, bringing corruption and death to the human species. So, the question is rhetorical: Satan is the author of dishonesty and is why transgression and evil exist.

Therefore, humankind's wicked personality is contrary to God's law, which affects every soul born of a woman. Immoral behavior surpasses the physical limits of humanity, mainly caused by a need for more material possessions. The causes and effects of materialism tell us we need expensive items, which may vex our Holy Spirit. To be less materialistic is to put time and effort into Christians with little. The simple desire for the material gain of sadistic pleasure does not overwhelm us.

Seek the Kingdom of God more than anything else, and live righteously, and he will give you everything you need Matthew 6: 33.

The Creator gave humans the power to make moral decisions according to God's commands or whatever they needed to sustain themselves. People are immortal but can accept JESUS, stay in Heaven for eternity, or go without salvation and live eternally in the underworld.

Thus, a human's natural tendency is an innate intelligence, exhibiting an intense level of insight. Or how to interpret that information and how we interact with humanity. People might disagree with others' spiritual convictions because of biased, wrong opinions. But our Christian ethos teaches us to respect the boundaries of everyone without compromising our sacred aims.

No other creature has as much psychological development and control over animals as humans. For example, humanity articulates speech and is upright in posture. The All-mighty made the homo sapiens' individualism to reason. So, their cognitive abilities, including language and intellectual skills, separate them from animals. Hence, their unique capabilities conduct functions other living organisms cannot.

- One, humans can effectuate an unlimited assortment of expressions and conceptions.
- They possess the intelligence to understand theological and secular connotations.

Despite Adam's and Eva's insubordination, Jehovah determined to make the homo sapiens in His Image and Likeness. From the foundation of the world, God wanted someone to fellowship with Him, the reason for humankind's creation. So, He initially granted Adam and Eva coequal privilege, dominion, and understanding conjointly with Him.

When the first parents acted in disobedience, they had the insight to understand their actions violated the Creator's Law. Still, they continued in disobedience by hiding their guilt. As the Genesis narrative continues, our efforts to cover our sinful actions cannot save us from our sinful nature. But in Jesus Christ's Atonement, we can recover from our bad choices.

So, across the globe, humans constitute God's fellowship of creation. We are the offspring of His righteous potentiality, or Holy spiritual beings in times to come. In Matthew 1:21, Jehovah sent His Only Son to Earth to save the sinful hominids from their misconduct. Therefore, through repentance of Jesus, the Father saves humanity from their incompetence. The Deity cleanses those who accept His righteousness, allowing them to be immaculate before the Blessed and only Ruler after their life ends on the planet.

Holiness is an acceptance and built-in resiliency that allows Christians to overcome challenging obstacles. But excluding (Jesus) the Offspring of David (Revelation 22: 16), is adhering to a disposition focused on rejecting the Supreme Sovereign grace. Dismissing Holy Nature as inappropriate won't affect church-goers' lives positively.

Note that every individual comes from one personage (Adam). So, humankind's intellectual/mental capacity and efficiency come from the first parents foremost. But now, through the death and resurrection of Jesus Christ, those who are righteous receive Godly intelligence. Refusal to recognize the high calling of the Head of the Church can lead to an individual's exclusion from the everlasting kingdom.

Thus, everything we have, and undoubtedly our individualities, are benefits from THE AUTHOR and PERFECTER of OUR FAITH. The homo sapiens' life becomes detached from God because of Adam's sin, resulting in body and spiritual fatality. So, we must repent our sins and accept The Hope of Glory as LORD and SAVIOR because no living soul can ever enter Heaven through their efforts and work.

Even though humankind is still intelligent, they are born separated from the Blessed and only Ruler in the Spirit. The Bible teaches that the assurance of redemption rests on the unshakable pillars of accepting Jesus as the Savior. Romans 10: 9.

The passage in Romans 5: 17-18 mentions how Adam's mistake led to a long-term wave of sin and evil among people, causing death to have dominion over billions. So, how can humanity deliver itself from the first parent's disobedience? The answer is that everyone must accept by faith the Great High Priest (CHRIST) (Ephesians 2: 8-9).

WHY? Three Scriptural Verses:

(1) He is the God-sent SAVIOR prophesied in Isaiah (chapter 35)
(2) He is Compassionate (Luke 7: 13-15)
(3) The Chief Cornerstone is the Sovereign and Powerful Holiness of the Universe (John 1: 1-3).

To understand THE LORD's humanity, we accept that the Faithful and True Witness is the Origin of Existence, taking away the world's sins. Thus, He is the ultimate sacrifice for humanity and deprived of the shedding of His Blood; no one can be responsible for immoral acts.

Charles Spurgeon said well: "You might live without Christ, but you can't die apart from Him."

Life's transformation is in Scripture. The Bible has had a significant effect on Western education and the economy. So, society has no excuse for its ungodliness. Psalm 141: 4 said: "Incline, not my heart to dishonorable words; to make excuses for my sinful nature." (See Romans 2: 1-29).

Ignorance poses an unjustifiable risk for the Saints. But no person develops moral qualities until they learn the value of submitting to Christ. Though, there is no excuse for being rebellious toward God's Word, which brings eternal misery to the insubordinate. Apostolic Education prevents followers from being vulnerable in situations.

Acknowledging our sins connects us to the Author of Life. Hence, He is THE KING of FAIRNESS who has made His Namesake known to generations, proving that he calls for supporters to learn of Him.

The fundamental lesson culture learns from scrutinizing the history of the Atoning Sacrifice for our Sins is that He is the Almighty's Son. There is ONE Sovereign Chief and unique mediator between Him and society, the Mortal Beginning and End, Who gave Himself as a payment to set everyone free (1 Timothy 2: 5-6).

Both the righteous and the unrighteous owe it to the Great Shepherd. We would not know our identity without Him coming into the flesh, as He has unchallenged sovereignty in the spiritual and physical realms (Matthew 28: 18-20). Understand Christian values through the Lord's mindset.

"Let this mind be in you, which was also in Christ:" This calls for the supporter's salvation by faith. The Glorified nature is the absolute certainty of having God's grace and mercy. The Saints can think like Alpha and Omega in a non-Jesus world.

CHAPTER 11

THE VALUE OF REPENTANCE

God showed His love for humankind by His Son's death. So, when an individual repents and becomes reborn in the Spirit, they qualify to spend infinity with Jehovah. The everlastingness of expenditures with the Alpha and Omega is the paramount goal of Christianity. So as the devoted, we should not fear death because the Saints have an afterlife waiting for them in an environment much better than what they have here.

But one CANNOT understand Holy Contrition living separately from THE HOPE in THE LAMB WITHOUT BLEMISH (1 Peter 1: 19). For Christians, nothing is more significant than entering Heaven after life on the planet. The faithful will experience an inexplicable manifestation of Glory. As a wedding ring circle exemplifies no end, so is the imperishability of self-responsibility and faith in Jesus.

Saints experience perpetual atonement and conviction. But belief in the Redeeming Holiness is essential for joy and contentment. So, while disciples remain on earth, asking for forgiveness is the platform for the Christlike to turn away from transgressions.

JESUS is the Infinite Atoning Sacrifice for the world's sins, the Mastermind Who washes a person's iniquities pure. His Love is a partition to keep any extraneous elements of intense contention between the homo sapiens and the Father. So, heartfelt contriteness quantifies humankind to avoid eternal fatality. That being so, it is impossible to receive salvation without confessing your immoral act to the Author of Life (John 14: 16).

JESUS CHRIST is the Lamb of the Godhead, and the prophet named Him Emanuel (MEANING GOD IS WITH US). He cast misdeeds as far as the East is from the West. Psalm 103: 12. His death and resurrection bring forgiveness. That is why we should know Him as our LORD and SAVIOR.

Yet, the value of self-contrition is the moral barometer for eternal life and the contributions we make to the lives of others to improve their positions. When a child of THE ALMIGHTY repents, it reforms their soul. For instance, eating a wide range of foods helps get the nutrients the body requires for good health.

Likewise, grace and mercy are vital spiritual minerals from God, Who created everything. And JESUS, Who taught us even better how to live. So, repentance grants homo sapiens overflowing assets to the whole of God's benefits. And when an individual embraces them, they understand a strengthening assortment of mercifulness.

The Man from Heaven allegory zeroed in on a diverse audience. For instance, the parable of the prodigal son shows the Creator's love and the power of asking for His forgiveness (see Luke 15: 11-32). The Great High Priest's bullet points below illustrate grace and mercy, recovering what seems impossible.

1. A DISPLACED SHEEP: representing innocence, fragility, and purity
2. A MISPLACED COIN: refers to unbelievers
3. A STRAGGLED AWAY SON: represents the forgiving Deity Almighty

The above allegories point to the celestial joy over every sinner who repents and turns to the Author of Life (Acts 3: 15). THE LORD was swift to speak the above apologue because the Pharisees and teachers of the Law were attacking him for embracing sinners and dining with them (Luke 11: 2).

Just so we are unmistakable, The Only Begotten Son does not condone sin. He, too, did not allow it to influence Him. To imitate JESUS, the Saints should stand firm enough on their faith to prevent worldly ideas from influencing their innate spirit. Again, the Author of Salvation did not avoid sinners—known in Biblical times as tax collectors.

Jesus cultivated relationships with sinners, communed with them, and shared supper with them. But one could only imagine what manner of vulgar expression THE LORD must have encountered with people who pretend to like Him. He sat at the supper table with Pharisees, who often indulge in hypocrisy. But He did not run from them. The Holy and True willingly stayed faithful toward Holiness.

James (5: 16) tells us to share our righteousness. Yet, we must first experience a conscience pricking pertinent to our misdeeds. How can disciples explain how repenting has helped them come closer to the Father if they cannot talk about their former life as a sinner?

1 Peter 3: 15-16 reads, "Always be prepared to answer everyone who questions you to give the reason for your belief. Execute this with tenderness and respect."

The phenomenon of authentic contrition to THE LORD is that it discharges personal liberation in their way of existence. But repentance is useless and void besides JESUS. We cannot change our sinful history. Without a pure heart and a clear sense of self, we will not advance in time because nothing is more common than exhortations to repentance.

To show misconduct to the Lion of the Tribe of Judah is a soul-searching moment of Godly reliance. But when we share our sins with somebody else and "intercede for each other," it gives us overcoming power to support each other wrong. So, we increase in righteousness and do more Christ-center as righteous people. Holiness is every disciple's aim. Thus, the Saints must confess their unethical behavior to another trusted believer, then pray for one another's healing.

Acknowledging our immoral acts to others is not just relevant to oneself; it benefits those with whom you tell your confession because it gives the hearers the bravery to unmask their righteous honesty. When members of a congregation routinely own up to their sins to one another, it creates a feeling of perseverance, benevolence, and pardon.

The Almighty needs His people to be submissive and acknowledge their wrongs. Relative to covering up shortcomings, contrition heals imagined and genuine offenses. Accepting mistakes creates self-healing.

So, repentance is Jehovah's intention for how Christians achieve forgiveness. The Firstborn, Over All Creation, is by what means He blesses His followers instead of cursing them for their unethical behaviors. His compassion for the undeserving is more than what is rightfully justifiable. Ephesians 2: 8 says, "For by grace He preserves, through faith, and that not of yourselves." So, Christian justification does not come from the Saint's works. The waters of true gracefulness are impure if we seek to mingle our efforts with God's kindness.

As for repentance, the Author learned mature Christians should take nothing for granted in Christian Education years ago. So, he shall not assume that every believer knows the value of asking the Father to forgive their sins. Remembering that, Bishop Bingham states the obvious; we repent by turning away from sin and surrendering our ways of life to the Almighty. We cease struggling to figure out our problems and allow THE LORD to offer us His agenda.

The Lamb Without Blemish is more than willing to teach the orthodox His purposefulness and strategy for their careers. But He also wants His people to show they know His intention, to design for creation, and follow it. So, He calls for supporters, at the least, to undertake His plan and atone when they sin. Accepting God's purpose can help wrongdoers view holiness. Life is challenging and full of responsibility.

But each moment the Saint commits themselves to The Author and Perfecter of Our Faith, they become more filled and governed by the Divine Spirit (Ephesians 5: 18). Following JESUS displays faith in Him. Submitting to THE LORD demonstrates a deep commitment to His Holiness; they can trust in His impact on their future and their unseen environment. Yet, Redemptive Adoration grows in the authenticity of true repentance. Ecclesiastical love is likewise a Holy contrast to the secular, inviting a sense of compassion and grace to those who visit the Local Church.

So, the virtuous may walk out in confidence despite the absence of evidence of their physical sensibility. Despite this, if the Glorified repents and follows the Infinite Spirit, He will never desert His followers or let them down if He guides them. The course might be uncertain; the climb could be shaky, and the descent could be great for one's wavering feet. Uncertainties and pitfalls are on every side. But when The Paraclete leads the Saints, they can trust His sacred willfulness to bring them to safety.

The Inhalation of Jehovah's Intercessor prepares and mentors everyone who laments and trusts Him (Acts 1: 5; John 14: 26; 16: 7). Jesus is The Horn of Salvation, Who fulfilled that promise in less than two weeks of His ascension. When an individual believes in Christ and repents their sins, the Breath of God instantly becomes an enduring part of their life after penitence (Romans 8: 14; 1 Corinthians 12: 13; Ephesians 1: 13–14). For instance, before the FIRSTBORN OVER ALL CREATION ascended to paradise, He advised His disciples He would assign the Holy Spirit to them. Then His Divine Will took authority over the believers at Pentecost (Acts chapter 2).

Repentance begins with THE LORD'S calling, then opening our minds to grasp His Message correctly. Then ask Him to help and study the Scripture to understand the need. The Saints must compare their beliefs, behavior, customs, traditions, and thoughts to the Hallowed Bible. Jehovah's Holy Writ is the only trustworthy standard by which supporters can measure their attitudes and conduct. Genuine self-accusation produces a change in the manner we live, even in the way we think.

The Authoritative Book tells us: "For if anyone is a listener of the word and not a doer, he is as a man observing his natural face in a mirror; for he observes himself, goes away, and at once forgets what sort of fellow he was. God blesses those who listen to the Perfect Law of Liberty and follow it by doing the work (James 1:23-25).

CHAPTER 12

THE AUTHENTICITY OF THE CHRISTIAN BIBLE SIMPLIFIED

Disbelievers in the Sacred Text believe that even Holiness's basic premise is beyond human understanding. But disciplines without a spiritual basis will be of no help to them. Although sometimes tremendously written, their traditional writings included unorthodox myths and cultural inaccuracies. Specifically, nonbelievers focus on the Christian Bible for what it is not - instead of what it is. Their limiting beliefs restrict them from knowing THE ALMIGHTY'S GENUINE NATURE.

Note the Holy Writ discloses the mysteries of our hearts straightforwardly. The Word of THE LORD is pure and shields from sin to everybody who takes refuge in it. The Authoritative Text originates in the Supreme Being, so its Consecrated Transcript is easy to comprehend, flawless, and with no flaws.

We can rejoice because the divine doctrines of the Bible are accurate. 2 Samuel 7: 28 tells us: "O Almighty Jehovah, You are the SAVIOR, and Your Words are truth, and You have promised this excellent thing to Your servant." See John 17: 17. But we should never interpret the Book of Books as our opinion. The human way of understanding replaces the sacred writings, undermining righteous faith's foundations.

Biblical interpretation should stand on the Scribe's intention of meaning and not the readers. So, we must consider the writer's context from a historical, grammatical, cultural, and literary perspective. To accomplish this task, we must use trustworthy theological research resources. A note, we are thousands of years removed from the Orthodox Text, and our history is distinct from theirs.

For a successful Christ-centered student, it is essential to possess a thorough study Bible. And a commentary that provides historical and cultural context. Most major translations come in editions with these transcripts, but the (New English Translation) excels most with over 60,000 notes. However, beware that most commentaries take a non-Christian or agnostic approach to God's work in history and method of studying the text.

The holy writings of Jehovah bring about a transformation in the soul that results in a moral change. Taking the intangible aspects of a person but not limited by the physical body. The Divine Writings can help Saints become better individuals and show their uniqueness. "You are My witnesses, says THE LORD," Isaiah 43: 10-12.

So, the Glorified words spread through life, and their mouths become tools for the Father's kingdom. The Book of Books shows the Author of Everything satisfies the lip with good things; thus, your youth renews as the eagles (Psalms 103: 5). Therefore, our acknowledgment of THE WORD will bring lasting recovery (Romans 10: 10).

Doctor Jocephus Bingham underlines the necessity of having a constructive outlook when reading the Bible. It can stimulate the brain to release beneficial hormones that lead to a brighter disposition. The Apostolic Testament encourages disciples to live an inward-to-outward life. The Scripture will guide believers to the understanding that being in the presence of the Almighty transforms the inner being and impacts outward expression, facilitating accessible communication of their beliefs.

Christianity is a noticeable and internal conviction; we love because the Messiah first loved us. So, the Presbyterian faith participates in daily living in a progressive and new intimate relationship with God.

Reading the Sacred Text enriches the writer's devotion to THE LORD. The scribe notes that non-compliant documentation induces negative feelings. The Holy Writ differs from non-Christian religious materials. Experiencing the power of the Scripture through reading them can provide a deep sense of contentment, peace, and intense joy.

Doctor Joecephus saw that pseudo-persuasion leads to different opinions on righteousness. Or suggest damaging modifications, disregarding Christ's teachings and creating conflict among loved ones.

Biblical teachings say that Jesus Christ's grace and mercy influence all life. For instance, humans usually follow their train of thought instead of the Almighty. The Bible instructs Saints to take a stand against corruption. Only THE HOLY BOOK of BOOKS teaches Jehovah's Word is the first concept of experiencing righteous joy and happiness, Nehemiah 8: 10.

Still, everybody transgresses, but the good that comes to the Glorified is the relationship they develop with the Atoning Sacrifice for Our Sins (1 John 2: 2). God's Word shows how to repent of sins.

But most unchristian materials adopt transgression's side instead of the Redeemer. They include all educational disciplines in non-religious intelligence, except Christianity. Rejecting Holy Script means not belonging to Him. Too, the rejectors of the Body of Christ enslave themselves to the sin of darkness. And unless they repent, Jesus will one day say to such people: "Depart from me." Matthew 7:21-23. "You have denied Me before men; I will also deny you before My Father."

Nonbelievers have seen the errors in formal writing, yet they still accept laxity over righteousness. The Pharisees were an example of this; they thought they could deceive God by using their established traditional religion as an excuse for sinning. They dressed up for their immoral activities and tried to appear devout and reverent among the parishioners. But James 1:17 tells the readers: "Every perfect gift is from above, coming from the Almighty of the heavenly lights, who does not resolve as shifting shadows."

Inarguably, we dishonor the Faithful Scrip by adding or subtracting from it. Too, we need not dress THE LORD'S Holy Writings up to make it sound better; the Bible has all the ability possible, including the " temporal " and "Sacred." So, we should not have to defend using "Secular" in content and context to prove a point. But turning it around becomes dysfunctional when we knowingly try to embellish it to match our opinion.

Outwardly, what we add to the Consecrated Writ sounds harmless with good intentions. But inwardly, it's working to deceive. For instance, the saying is true, "Putting silk socks on a pig is useless because the first mud hole he sees, he will get in it." Adding to God's Word, it's like stepping into a pagan's mudhole dressed in religious garments.

1 Corinthians 6:20 shows: "For Jesus bought humanity with the price of His Blood. Blending human theories with Biblical teachings on salvation lessens the message. However, the Authoritative Book explicitly encourages us to learn from other sources, yet we should filter what we read and hear through the Bible. And nobody has the authority to change the Good News Doctrine. But to understand it at face value, we exalt THE FATHER with the quality of our being. So, the Holy Writ is clear: "We belong to THE LORD."

We serve the Faithful and True Witness-holistically. Deuteronomy, 4: 2, "You shall not add to The Word which I command you, nor remove anything from it" (also Deuteronomy 12: 32). The reason God is so immobile on this is that "the entire Bible is the truth." History has validated the Devout Book compared to other renowned writers and their literature.

Therefore, Matthew 5: 16 is unambiguous: "Let your light shine before men, that they may look upon your good works, and glorify the Alpha and Omega in heaven." But if a person tries to dress up the Holy Writ with their ideology, they can no longer obey God's commands, for they have altered His interpretation with their own. Proverbs 30: 6 says, "Do not add to His Words, lest He rebukes you, and others see you as a liar."

The Saints who categorically understand the very essence of THE LORD is Love. So, when we rightly interpret The Word of Yahweh, there is harmony between the Sacred Writings and them. We share intimacy with His Holy Text and can be deep-spirited friends with the Father because it roots us in Him. Yet, no agreement exists among the thousands of universal nontheist religions relevant to who or What THE DIVINE BEING is. But most false doctrines teach paganism and believe in the big bang theory genre while proclaiming Allah's unity.

Christians maintain that the Spirit of Yahweh is all-powerful and omnipresent. And they rejoice in every outlook of Christ's Holy Sovereignty. King David said, "THE SUPREME BEING has established his throne in Heaven" (2 Samuel chapter 7). And so, disciples need not argue unmindfully responding to His existence. Still, the All-Knowing wants His followers to be intelligent when sharing their righteousness.

Everyone who reads the Bible should behave as simply as smiling. So, we should more willingly confront our preconceptions in righteousness than prove problems without a doubt. Christians can pray for themselves and others by understanding Scripture well. So, supporters should seek ways to administer the Divine Doctrine intelligently.

Too, arguing to prove the Scripture does not help; it sabotages one's witness (2 Timothy 2: 14). Just because we cannot lay eyes on the

Heavenly Father does not mean He does not live. Scientists have proven it; unseen gases, air, and electricity are nonfictional.

Likewise, "when the male semen meets the female Ovum, her egg becomes fertilized. And in time, a baby comes to life." "The microscopic objects an individual can see with sight are 0.1 millimeters, and sperm come in at 0.05 fraction. During the development of fertilization, the oval is discernible in the human eye, but the masculine seed is not." So too, not seeing the Humble Spirit is not a reason to accept the Alpha and Omega should not exist.

However, the Bible proves once a person is (born again John 3: 16), the Holy Presence is alive in the physical body. The Blood of the Savior covers them to do good. A righteous change takes place in the heart. JESUS CHRIST stated, "A healthy plant cannot foster rotten produce, nor will a deficient tree bear useful fruit."

An individual either has hopefulness (belief void of proof) or chooses not to understand (simplified). Specifically, nobody in their human form can prove the existence of the Inhabitance of the Creator (*The Bible state God is*). One must have faith in the Breath of Jehovah to be in a relationship with THE FIRSTBORN OVER ALL CREATION.

"One must believe in coming to the Almighty" (Hebrews 11: 6).

To authenticate the Bible, we must use verifiable truths and build validation that links different facts. For instance, the ultimate source of the entire universe proves certainty that God's Word causes the effect unseen. And the intuitive thought of humankind's reasoning, THE LORD, created them in His image.

THE AUTHOR and PERFECTER of OUR FAITH have called His people to be populations of the Scripture. The Divine Book writers never set out to prove the existence of the Holy Messiah. AGAIN, THEY SPECIFY THAT GOD IS. They understood Jehovah's goal with evidence and intention. Socially, we care for one another. So, the indoctrination of the homo sapiens' heart is the Father's responsibility. But the evangelical duty is to study to divide His truth rightly.

So, disciples are to witness the Gospel with kindness and regard; there are opportunities everywhere around believers to share their intellectual faith. Quarreling over God's Word diminishes trust. Christian misconduct only moves to blaming, criticizing, and defensiveness is troublesome. Unprofessional believers' behavior destroys relationships, a sense of safety, and security.

For instance, when Paul arrived in Athens's metropolis, he passed by a shrine with the inscription of the hundreds of gods they worship. The Apostle understood that every lost person deserves eternal salvation. Unbelievers are "not yet" followers of the Firstborn From the Dead (Revelation 1: 5). The Bible encourages supporters to help transgressors know THE LORD JESUS CHRIST, not to ridicule them. Our innate spirit should always seek to guide our friends and family toward Christ.

But we must be prayerful and non-threatening. Paul addressed Areopagus' "Undisclosed Deity." "TO THE UNKNOWN GOD" (Acts 17: 23). The evangelists used their subtitles to introduce the Holy Christ. He taught them the New Testament teachings.

Paul, too, enlightened the Athenians, responding to the ANONYMOUS IMMORTAL about their gods. He had them understand the Undisclosed Deity was the Horn of Salvation. The Son of Jehovah is an objective reality for all humanity. Pagans and Christians examine Him and prove Him acceptable.

Too, Paul abundantly stated that the Offspring of David is without sin (Hebrews 4: 15). God's Son humbly gave up His divinity to experience life with people.

The evangelist explained how THEIR UNKNOWN JEHOVAH is THE AUTHOR of LIFE. Thus, He can empathize and comfort humankind through sorrow because He experienced humanity's grief on the cross. Throughout the Old and New Testaments, JESUS is the same as humans. Although He is a Unified Person with Individual but has Divine Attributes. Specifically, He is the Word of God.

The former Pharisee Orator kept informing them that the UNKNOWN Deity, or "Un-Greek." Jesus is the Nazarene, listed last on their Religious Directory. The Divine chroniclers recorded 100+ Bible affirmations about the Creator's nature. Then furnish supplementary details about the Nazarene's title and divine intent. And how THE LORD disregarded people's illiteracy in earlier times relevant to His Identification, but there is no excuse these days.

Again, the Subheads of JESUS are essential because God saves humankind through the Son of David's death, burial, and resurrection. He is teaching them that (He is the Root of David Revelation 5: 5; 22: 16), yet He is "The Maker of EVERYTHING.

The Bible's Preeminence Titles of the Blessed and Only Ruler enable people to understand the SAVIOR better. For example, JESUS' Inscriptions show the prophecy of the return of the One Mediator (1 Timothy 2: 5) to earth at the Last Judgment. He has not come back sooner because the Consecrated Father is allowing individuals a chance to repent, turn from their sins, and escape the coming wrath.

Immanuel's divine and human nature allowed Him to end eternal death. So, THE SON'S Mystery is an immeasurable promise by Jehovah for humanity; it is the Second Advent of the Prince of Peace that the world expects.

In Acts 17, verse thirty tells us: "The seasons of insensitivity the Holy One overlooked in former time. Paul links our unholy circumstances to the Good Shepherd." What does this chapter show believers today? That the age of ignorance has ended! Humanity's salvation was a secret for hundreds of years. But the Head of the Church has uncovered mysteries surrounding eternal redemption, so nobody has an excuse to die in sin.

Because of JESUS' sacrificial death, everyone who accepts His redeeming quality is heir to His righteousness Acts 2: 38. Every supporter simultaneously is of one body and shares jointly in the promise of the Redeemer. So, as we read Acts chapter 17, we learn the Apostle's insight into the subtlety of Christ. Other past generations were void of understanding. Yet, the Spirit has now disclosed it to God's righteous Saints. Christ's Divine Humility works in the Glorified to make them what the Father would have us to be.

Paul's philosophical insights at Mars Hill helped the crowd understand God's power. Still, He had them know; He is the SAVIOR over the hundreds of gods on their official roster.

For instance, Paul wrote to the Philippians, "And my God shall supply each need according to His riches in Glory by Christ Jesus (Philippians 4: 19, 20). Whether their condition is spiritual or physical, He will not withhold any good thing from the righteous (Psalms 84: 11). But the Prince of Peace commands all nations to repent their sins and turn to Him for salvation. Acts 17: 30.

Paul's reprimand included " every human being." The statement excludes no individuals. And "everywhere" implies not where they might live. The dark part of the world, He incorporated. We have no excuses for embracing evil. Everyone is guilty and deserves the wrath of the Holy and True. If we sin deliberately after receiving the knowledge of the truth, there no longer remains a renouncing for immoral acts. Hebrews 10: 26.

Every mortal knows the reality of the matter of Jehovah. But sometimes, we do wrong because we have a sinful nature, which affords no excuse to make unacceptable choices. But as believers, the Atoning Sacrifice for our Sins offers His people a choice. Yet, His Holy Spirit encourages the Saints to do the right thing. Knowledge of the King of kings did not just happen spontaneously. Besides, He is The Redeemer Who provides for the Glorified through reasoning and everything they need to be fruitful and multiply.

Hosea 4: 6 tells the reader: "People destroy themselves when voiding of Christian education." Destruction is a wide-wasting desolation when the Saints do not study to show themselves approved. Listen, when anyone rejects the wisdom of the Bible, they are without understanding.

THE LORD chastens the righteous because they banish His enlightenment. He will soon reprimand them when their carnal mind becomes enmity against Him (Romans 8: 7). *Confucius said: "Real knowledge is to know the extent of one's ignorance."* Because we are Christians does not mean we have the basics of freedom to live the same as brainless nincompoops.

A deeper understanding of the Bible and its prophetic revelations can be helpful through Christian Education. But we must study the Book of Books, which supports the Saints to advance in faith and holiness. The Word encourages supporters to secure in the Messiah by exploring His unsealed Holy Dogma.

The Sacred Writings show God's plan for a believer's life as they eat the hidden manna, feeding on the Good Shepherd's Pure Writ (John 6: 57). So, feasting on His Manuscript teaches us to abide in Him beyond secular impractical. Disciples must continue to remember THE LORD of RIGHTEOUSNESS. He is more powerful than the devil. So, making JESUS CHRIST SAVIOR, the Scripture's indoctrination, gives the Glorified security in His Hope of Glory.

The saying is true: "Knowledge is the treasure of a wise man" (anonymous). Christian Discipline is the most potent gift Jehovah has given the Righteous to change a sinful atmosphere. The Sacred Text teaches disciples relevant to the HOLY MORTAL living within us. Colossians 1:10 says to walk in a way that pleases and bears fruit for THE LORD.

The primary step to please the Resurrection and Life (John 11: 25) is "walking in the Spirit." "Then we must continue by faith" (Hebrews 10: 38). The Mediator of the New Covenant (Hebrew 9: 15) cannot satisfy those who "retreat to their former pastime of sin." Finally, act responsibly before Non-Christians and perpetuate sexual purity. Christian Education teaches followers to know the will of the Last Adam. The Bible shows believers how to renew their minds. Romans 12: 2 tells them not to conform to the pattern of this world. We should bring righteous fruit into every work to grow in God's knowledge.

Our Redemption created humankind to have a relationship with Him and be alive with purpose. The Father's Writ guides Christians to evaluate behavior individually. Staying true to Christian Education directs believers to take a dedicated route instead of pretending to be Christian.

The absence of authentic redemption is a fundamental problem in apostolicism. Romans 12:11 says, "Not lagging in diligence, fervent in spirit, serving THE LORD." The Verse shows us how important to stay diligent in Christ. A believer who does not study cannot equip and mobilize sinners and the Saints to share the truth and love of Our Precious Cornerstone (1 Peter 2: 6) worldwide. Listen, only the Gospel respects this life and eternity!

JESUS, the Prince of Peace, came to the earth with a message of hope filled with noble possibilities for humanity. The Apostle taught that faith in the sacrifice of the Messiah results in righteous assurance laid up for them in Heaven. Jehovah requires an ethical faith in the SAVIOR, enabling humans to coexist eternally as God's children in the Old and the New Testament.

Not to be redundant, but it is why Paul said in Acts 17: 22-23, "Now, what you idolize as something nameless, I will declare to you." In the meeting of the Areopagus, the Apostle's lecture spoke of the UNKNOWN GOD and the Supreme Being who created and controlled them.

So, these Pagan educators' understanding was open using the Scripture. Paul showed the Bible, declaring that the Author of Redemption is the SAVIOR of the World. He is the Creator of the planet and the universe. And He brings salvation from the consequences of legalism to hope in the Atoning Sacrifice for Our Sins. Romans 6: 23 says, "For the wages of sin is death, but the gift of THE LORD is eternal life in Christ."

Since they printed the Biblical Creed centuries ago, the Bible is still the world's leading-selling Book. Yet most nonbelievers are not likely to understand the incredible writing. But devotion to Scripture can help you exceed your tremendous achievements and dreams. Gaining Canonical knowledge gives life satisfaction. Then the Christian lives are rich and meaningful, complete with righteous hope.

The Apostle Peter said, in the same way, that recent babies crave the pure spiritual cream so that by it you shall grow up in your salvation. For instance, a mother's breast milk has every nutrient a child needs to jump-start growth.

Adults benefit from vitamins, minerals, antioxidants, flavonoids, and phytonutrients from fruits and vegetables. Hence, the birth of a newborn is simply the beginning point. However, a child leaves the preliminary stages of life, then develops and grows into a strong human until adulthood. Hence, anatomy requires more meats and grains of cuisines for a vital piece of a healthy diet.

Jehovah's plan for sinners who give their life to Christ is that they advance powerfully in His Doctrine. The same is typical for baby Christians. They are sacred newborn babies after accepting JESUS' redemption but are not to stay in that condition. So, we get the "pure

Divine milk" through reading and studying the Holy Writ through shared worship practices.

Like communion and prayer, the Apostolic Church can collaborate with other Christian faiths. The Bible teaches Christian companionability builds up in the faith. Acts 2: 42-47, Hebrews 10: 25. Staying true to righteousness requires a regular focus on Scripture and incorporating God's Word into one's life.

So, the milk of Scripture spawns solemn development. But as believers grow spiritually, the body craves more rich food from the Sacred Text. When one or both are missing from Christianity's diet, it will stunt growth. 1 Peter 2: 2. The only way to get the sincere cream and ample manna from Heaven is to read the Word.

The Book of Books brings solace and understanding. Strengthening faith through consistent Bible study is part of righteousness.

A human craving is a strong feeling of wanting something. Distractions and desires prevent God's people from concentrating on the Gospel. Then mental distress keeps the mind wandering to the unnecessary and not paying attention to the sermon or Biblical teaching. We should cast away those unrighteous elements, stopping the Saints from receiving THE LORD'S Dialog.

So, unknowledgeable and freedom cannot coexist simultaneously in the Holy integrity realm. Godly insight destroys ignorance as light overcomes intense darkness. The brilliant light of the Word allows believers to prove righteous ideas and generate results for problems. Avoiding sinful decisions because of ignorance leads to a moral future. Ignoring divine wisdom and relying on sophisticated understanding shows a lack of submission to God.

For example, The Apostle Paul's Letter to the Romans rebukes their foolishness. "For they are being ignorant of God's uprightness. They show hominid faithfulness by not submitting themselves to the Morality of the Blessed and only Ruler. He is the Chief Cornerstone and the end of a human mandate for virtuousness to everyone who believes."

Moses describes righteousness in the Pentateuch as the Law, and the individual who obeys it shall continue with it. Romans 10: 3-5. To live by the Almighty's Word means the person has humbled himself under the mighty Hand of JESUS CHRIST. For example, in the eighth chapter of Deuteronomy, the man who parted the Red Sea advises Israel: never forget to recognize the Everlasting Father. Forgetting involves a failure in the memory to retrieve knowledge from the Bible relevant to Holiness.

CHAPTER 13

CHRISTIAN UNAWARENESS

Educating oneself is possible through a variety of methods. Acquiring true wisdom, however, requires respect and reverence for THE LORD. And admiration for His grace and mercy and obedience to His commands. Yielding is a Christian moral judgment and decision-making to allow the Almighty to fight your battle. Submitting to God will reduce toxic stress.

Besides, surrendering oneself to the authority of Holiness is the principle of proper behavior for the Glorified. That is why moralistic cognition is one of the ultimate core values the Church should seek. Certain believers think they understand Theological Documents better than Jesus, but they are wrong.

But brainy broadcasting how smart you are is a form of transgressing against God's Deity. Allow others to express your accolades, not yourself. Those who boast about their academic success and advertise their superiority, THE LORD sees them as unstable and merely pretending. Boastful individuals are likely to have low self-esteem and veiled ambiguity; habitually, they try to cover up their weak faith in Jesus Christ.

So, self-important, on any level, contrasts the Divine Being's authoritative order (study Acts 12: 23). People who show off show spiritual narcissism, exaggerating their material needs and desires (as described in 1 Corinthians 3: 1-3). The word carnal translates from the Greek expression sarkikos, meaning "fleshly."

The people mentioned above claim to be knowledgeable but are gossipy, arrogant people who can't take pleasure in anything around them. They talk profusely, especially in a bold or antagonistic manner. They are often presumptuous, judgmental, and critical.

To have as a neighbor someone who refuses to understand their inadequacies is fatiguing. Only the ignorant think they know what is best for them. But they are insolent and only prove how their vanity engenders their absurdity, which leads to cognitive bias. If Christians heed the advice of the unenlightened and impious, these earthly, sinful creatures will ruin a good day. Since they misinterpret Gospel information, how can they rationalize right and wrong Christian dogmas?

The soul void of Biblical knowledge has a limited understanding of the nonphysical. Lacking righteous incomprehensiveness gives birth to both mental and superstition. These together are vehicles for the typical antagonist of humanity. Their influence is bred-in-the-bone in the willful illiteracy not to obey the Messiah's commandment to research the Holy Writ. Yet, their disobedience causes torment and death to millions of individuals every year at the hands of fellow humans. Ignorance of His Word brings spiritual darkness.

Besides, those who frown on God's average duties often stem from their willingness to take on minor tasks. However, arrogant Saints believe unimportant Christian aim and obligations cause them unhappiness. Helping those who face limitations is a serious responsibility we should not ignore. Any mission from THE LORD is sacred to overcoming various obstacles. And they shall keep us rejoicing in doing good with joyfulness unrestricted.

Zechariah 4:10 - "For who has despised the day of small things?"

Even with trivial tasks, Jehovah will perform meaningful results from unimportant items. For instance, The Firstborn, Over All Creation, asked the confused Moses standing at the Erythra Thalassa, "What is that you got in your hand?" He replied, "My walking stick." Our Holiness said, "Stretch it out," "And then the Red Sea parted. Exodus chapter 10." So, has God challenged you to do something seemingly meaningless that you have not yet attempted to achieve? "Do not despise these small beginnings, for the Lord rejoices to see the work begin," Zechariah chapter 4.

Likewise, even the most righteous often ignore the importance of the modest works of JESUS. But the influence of undersized assignments may be of great relevance for good and is exceptional when conducted for THE CHURCH GROWTH (John 6: 1-14). A subnormal mission's single-mindedness develops into a significant harvest of blessings when we allow God to use them for His Glory. Therefore, "The somebody we trust with small duties is trustworthy with much. But the person who is dishonest with little will also be deceitful with considerable." Luke 16: 10.

Season Saints understand Christlikeness means reacting to His Authority and living within His Righteousness. Holiness encourages risk-takers and bold Saints to take a chance despite the negative connotation, even if the work may not be fulfilling to them. The Glorified must be courageous people, not someone filled with dread. Mature Saints do not scare easily and do not decide based on anxiety. The veteran believer looks forward to their future without fear of what imperilment ensues.

But fears drive immature Christians. Instead of trusting the Divine Spirit or working through problems by the Consecrated Writ of The Faithful and True Witness (Revelation 3: 14). They justify everything by saying: "That is extremely too demanding," or "I do not choose to," or "I have to pray foremost for this crisis." We should always petition The Supreme Being and never give up hope. Jesus told His supporters to pray and not to lose heart (Luke 18: 1). We, too, must devote ourselves to intercession and search for concrete ways to remedy the challenges.

We grow through prayer and acting on the Great High Priest's Authority; the two concepts work together. Accepting and appreciating the light missions in life means focusing on what nurtures and sustains us. Besides, everything we do and see has a limited beginning. The ocean - is tiny drops of water. THE LORD created humans from small grains of dirt. Case in point, do enough minor tasks, and they add up to greatness.

Untruth and fear block the Glorified from the Holy Spirit's position. But when we confront our negative attributes, we gain power, while anxiety loses strength. Too, neglecting Christian duty is trepidation for believers afraid to take risks. The only steppingstone to overcoming uneasiness and mental incapacity is confronting them in the Word of THE LORD. Then we embrace the challenge and rise to the occasion to solve it, which allows us to be open about our feelings with The Supreme Being.

Prayer and works are minor attributes of Christians. But ignoring God's simple request shows the Saint has no honest insight. A note snubbing off meager assignments displays a little passion for others or a lack of attention to Divine obligations. The irony is that they feel mistreated when the Author of Salvation reprimands them for being uninterested.

But chastening comes to correct guilty feelings or unpleasant circumstances. Accept the chastisement of THE LORD, keep your composure, and acknowledge His assessment. Without God's feedback, it's just someone's reaction to your skills.

Listen, ignorance assumes what never happened and in no sense could be. The devastating issue of Christian unawareness forbids the Saints from adhering to the Messiah and not bypassing sin. Then wrongdoing leads to more iniquity, and transgressions imprison a Saint to the totality of intents and nothing more.

The strongest disciples lose their respect and self-esteem when they realize they are on the path of ignorance because of corruption. The phrase is widespread: "Everything that glitters is not gold." Chasing the glitter of illiteracy appeals directly to the flesh, with no regard for the expenses of dishonesty.

For example, King David was an individual after THE LORD'S Heart. As Christians today, THE LORD blessed him to understand His Command. Jesus said throughout the Gospels, "He that has ears to hear, let him listen!" Matthew 11: 15, 13: 9, and 13: 43. Had this son of Jesse listened and obeyed the Holy Spirit, the devastating tide of adultery with Bathsheba could not have happened.

David's dishonor breached trust, and the transgression of confidentiality wreaked destruction in his kingdom. The entangled betrayal affair for everybody is always the result of an affection shortfall in marital communication. Specifically, for David:

1. A baby was born and died from David's sin
2. Amnon raped his sister, Tamar
3. The suffering of Jehovah's people
4. The Blood cost of the Almighty's Son on the cross

God's king should have known sleeping with another man's wife was wrong. Fleeting sensual pleasure separates the Saints from God. When the thrill is gone, they realize the suffering is about more than just infidelity. Besides, years later, David's son wrote: "He who commits adultery lacks sense; he who does it destroys himself (Proverbs 6: 32)."

Pastors and leading evangelists who expose themselves to inquisitive immorality will tell us. They would never repeat the same mistake if they knew the pain it caused.

Broken Christian influence may not be simple to restore. The Saints must constantly defend their faith. Restoring a respected reputation after an act of unfaithfulness is difficult. Yet it is achievable through sustained patience, commitment, and determination. Still, sometimes the damage to your good name is no liability of yours, but in infidelity, the Bible tells the readers. "He who commits adultery lacks sense; he who does it destroys himself" Proverbs 6: 32.

Absolution allows access to the Redeemer and freedom from retribution. When a disciple is honest, their life conforms to the Gospel of JESUS CHRIST; THE LORD'S Eyes are on them; His Ears are receptive to their prayers. 1 Peter 3: 12; Proverbs 15: 9.

So, doing the right thing is a vital state of mind that combines the big three concepts for the Glorified: talents, emotions, and judgment. The Saints who rely on worldly experience alone are risky, given how swiftly physical and sexual needs can change. But under the banner of Holiness, they are much more correct than "gain and loss" of temporal pleasure and mundane reasoning.

Albeit immoralities cause the faithful to lose the zeal for a righteous life. Besides, Lucifer strikes Christians where they lack: giving in to the absence of faith. Despite their lack of virtuous behavior and honor, they remain connected to Jehovah, but Lucifer has weakened their faith.

The hidden failure of adultery was David's troubles independently. But God still loved Him! Yet, his transgression causes him companionship with THE LORD for a year (see Psalm 63). The choice for anyone to sin is not THE LORD'S or Satan's fault. The Apostle James instructed the supporters too, "Yield to the Almighty. Resist the devil, and he will flee from you" (James 4: 7).

Despite this, the Bible tells the righteous: "Everybody has sinned and fallen short of the Glory of Jehovah." Romans 3: 23, and that "the wages of sin are death." Romans 6: 23. But the Supreme Being has provided humankind with the remedy for transgressions in His Divine Writ (Repent).

The Almighty provides followers a new life of salvation, vested by the Hallowed Spirit to overcome evil. So, when a Saint trespasses, they must confess their misdeeds to the Messiah and accept his forgiveness. Repentance brings us closer to righteousness, humbles us, and drives away imps.

Satan's functionaries command temptation. Therefore, the Almighty warned His followers in the Pentateuch against false doctrine. See Jeremiah 29: 8 and 1 John 2: 21. God tells the Testament Saints they are imperishable individuals canonized by THE BRIDE of JESUS (the Church) and devoted to Sainthood. Christians commit themselves to worship and serve the ONE TRUE SUPREME JEHOVAH, revealed in Jesus, the Savior.

But supporters of the SAVIOR are not safe from the devil's deception. So, "Be sober, be watchful: your adversary the devil, as a roaring lion, walking, and seeking whom he may devour," 1 Peter 5: 8.

Scripture teaches us widespread accessibility and the Redeemer's Sovereignty. By understanding God's moral will, believers gain a code of ethics from interpreting His Son's revelation. His Truthful Integrity is then Ecclesiastical. THE LORD'S Hallowed veracity leads the Glorified to fruitful action.

Realism becomes instrumental content for the Saints. So, Holiness for humanity has the holistic value of truthfulness. Christian's salvation is of JESUS CHRIST. And He listens to His disciples. Whoever is not from the Creator does not listen to Him. Divineness is how we recognize the Temperament of Righteousness and the heart of falsehood. 1 John 4: 6.

Regardless, independent Christianity is becoming a rarity in our Christian society because of deceitfulness. For instance, someone's predecessor told them to believe in a Deity because their parents raised them that way. So, besides regular Worship attendance, disciples must study for themselves. Faith in what the Bible says means trusting God's Holy Writ is the truth. As often as we read the Word of God, He imparts to the Saints revelation of knowledge. The belief that THE LORD started in us will increase when subjected to His Good Book.

For instance, a baby Saint might be hopelessly uneducated responding to the genuine meaning of righteousness. Still, their conviction and works must justify no one besides God for His grace and mercy. So, Christian morality belongs to The Creator of Everything. He only is the Lawgiver manifested in His Laws. When we hear the Gospel, we should investigate it for the journey of growing in faith (Acts 17: 11).

Skill teachers understand apprentices need more than lectures to comprehend the subjects thoroughly. So, educators send students home with homework to improve academic performance and foster life skills. Too, household devotion to Scripture is much more than completing an assignment. It establishes righteous behavior skills to support them throughout daily living. The Biblical study improves time management, resource control, and communication.

Self-follow-up research strengthens mental and moral qualities. Divine Text homework helps the bibliophile comprehend obedience and disobedience.

Besides, Biblical home study gets THE LORD of Lords Involved in the family and teaches effective planning. Sacred Writing's exploration leads bibliolatrist about righteous familiarity.

Faith is magnificent when a personal relationship between a believer and THE LORD is constant. Noble-minded Christians live according to the Lamb of God in the Ancient Biblical Text. But Satan has rigged the world's order to serve the powerful. So, affluent sinners often brag about their bias. Alternately, individual wealth absent of Christ determines how they understand the world.

Mental prejudice leads people to interpret information to favor their beliefs. Judging the destitute to annotate somebody's flaws, they dismiss their feelings and experiences. The Head of the Church should witness the Word to the loss and give to the underprivileged without show or approval. So, when Jehovah blesses, believers must not consider the less successful inferior to suppose they are better than them.

Harboring judgmental behavior against the unknowledgeable becomes an obsession that makes Saint's righteousness noxious. Criticizing humankind for who they are or the insufficient of what they have is a personal attack. Sin is invariably the issue, not the living soul or their lack of prosperity. The Spirit-filled person does not look for fault in everybody because they are one with JESUS CHRIST.

Unfair criticism of an individual in The Prince of Peace provokes bitterness and diminishes trust in a righteous message. So how could anybody ever sway somebody to re-wire the intellect to love a God predicated on one's biased accusation? No condemnation of those in the Redeemer, regardless of their living standard. They walk not conforming to the flesh but affirming the Supreme Being." The decree of the Spirit of existence in The Galilean (JESUS) has set me free from the Law of sin and death (see Romans 8: 1-39).

CHAPTER 14

CHURCH AFFILIATION

Doctor Bingham failed to understand his spiritual outlook, despite his faith. Besides joining the Christian congregation, he considered himself compassionate, generous, and resourceful. He was relentless in advocating and addressing injustice.

Although apart from the Local Church membership. When someone asks how he would describe himself, he says: "An energetic big-hearted Godly individual who loves helping people." However, spiritual maturity and progressive conformity to the image of growing in Christ were absent from him.

The congregation helped Doctor Bingham understand uncertain times. He realized the world was constantly changing, and no one could pass through the unethical terrain without the guidance of the Church.

The wordsmith joyfully served others by learning Christian Doctrine. Through Church Affiliation, redemptive deliverance is always at the top of his list. Since joining the House of Worship, he inscribes his personal life within a Holy, elevated vocation to develop every dimension of his person. The writer finds his identity rooted in his relationship with the Author of Salvation.

Precisely, conscience thought in the Devout aspects of Jesus' identity has led to a greater understanding of the writer's inner self. He stays active in prayer with others and reading the Word to stand against the devil's schemes (Ephesians 6: 11). So, because of a Divine connection with the Saints, there is less conflict and the ability to sustain caused by evil.

The Body of Christ's highest insight tells who we are in The Blessed and Only Ruler. And he understands that his belief is important enough to give up His Life for his canonized ethical convictions. Thus, constructive collaboration helps the wordsmith stay true to his principles, goals, and needs.

Humans often define themselves through their attitudes, capabilities, and situation. Church affiliation teaches that Jesus Christ alone has a permanent personality, as emotions can change. Sacred Stimulus can prompt swift changes in our physical and mental states, culminating in an emotional response. Emotions are constantly interacting with other emotions.

Besides, psychologists call the writer's generous spirit noted above "pro-social behavior." Or conduct that is constructive, supportive, and intended to encourage communal recognition and friendship. Ecclesiastical collaboration enhances personality and righteous expression.

Regrettably, no individual has clever solutions to helping individuals with their problems. It is an intricate work. Revealing a novice's true nature too quickly could cause anxiety. And that is frightening for them because it involves the possibility of irrevocable heartbreak that stirs up a surge of early sinful hormones. Therefore, the Church leadership must acknowledge the newcomer's tender feelings.

Still, we will find no one-size-fits-everybody answer when unmasking someone's wrongs relevant to the House of Prayer. However, people's distinct personalities meet the requirements to improve or disapprove of one's approaches. Yet, Christians can remove any panic in JESUS' Name when the Holy Spirit lives within an individual.

Whether a novice or mature Christian, pridefulness may rebut our friendly effort to help us overcome our fear; however, the Divine Father will make basic knowledge to pinpoint and resolve problems. But the Saints must come together unified in considerable prayer and compassion. Then witness the Most-High converting the disbelievers' hearts to attend Church.

THE LORD'S HOUSE is the groundwork for everyone to grow a meaningful and fulfilling existence. Again, the author's Church affiliation has enhanced his core values and passions. His moral principles and lifestyle are still flawed, but no perfect religions exist outside the Teachings of Christ. Christianity alone claims Jesus is God, with evidence from its writings and history. The truth of Jesus' resurrection implies Christianity is true.

So, Faith Formation is still suitable for the wordsmith. Now it has become an authorization for him to seek others and help develop their untapped talent for Christ (Matthew 28: 18-20) regardless of age or race. Besides, the Scripture mandates the laity should always unify to train the next generation of supporters. So, when Churchgoers come together, it must be for the underlying value to discover Humility—making JESUS the prosperity of morality. The Glorified should see humanity as righteous seeds, watching them germinate for Holiness' sake.

"Now I beseech you, brethren, by the Name of Our Lord, that we speak the same thing and that there be no divisions among you. But that you be perfect and on one accord by joining simultaneously in the same mind and judgment" (1 Corinthians 1:10). The Apostle Paul is helping the problematic believers at Corinth understand the Christian Church centers on Christ. Thus, Christianity is the belief in Jesus' Deity. Putting THE SON of GOD first makes it so easy to put life holistically into perspective.

The Agnostic Theist believes in a Supreme Being without ascribing to anyone's religion. Being a Christian without being associated with a particular Local Church is possible. Not joining the congregation can detract from an essential part of GOD's plan for faithful gatherings.

Exemplar, the writer of Hebrews, tells the Saints never to stop meeting. "And let the supporters consider how we may stimulate toward love and good deeds, not giving up gathering together" (Hebrews 10: 24-25).

Without the guidance of the Church, Christians outside the Apostolic faith cannot access their full potential. Though righteous, their Holiness only reveals a small part of the Gospel, leaving them open to incorrect beliefs rooted in human perfection.

Satan twists the apostate Saint's expectations and entangles their confidence. Believers need to spread their faith and grow in Christ together. Growing in THE LORD together is essential; it encourages us to produce good works and helps us to comprehend God's will. Therefore, maturity causes both Christians and non-Christians to follow this requirement. Since joining can help each one of us to strengthen our faith.

Again, no picture-perfect Churches exist in this life. "If somebody ever discovers any, do not enter them because you will ruin them!" Still, sinners, "God's grace saves us " (Ephesians 2: 8-9). Likewise, the Saints have no provocation to prove or measure their righteousness to anyone outside the congregation. Because when an individual knows their identity in the Alpha and Omega (Revelation 1: 8; 22: 13), they undertake to satisfy Him.

Also, there is no reason to equal themselves to anybody in the Church. Everyone stands on an even surface with the Author of Salvation, whether novice or mature. The Psalmist tells us, "Our feet stand on level ground; in the great congregation, and we will praise THE LORD" Psalm 26: 12.

The controversy of Holiness has been ongoing since the birth of The Disciples. Yes, it disheartens the Firstborn over all creation to see territorial and righteousness disputes among the assembly. Yet, the places of worship are influential because they show God's physical incarnation. But not being part of a faith community limits the understanding of Christianity.

However, no one needs to attend a basilica or upraised building to be a believer. But a devoted supporter of THE SAVIOR will recognize the need for the Body of Christ to gain wisdom by connecting with other kingdom builders. Too, joining a Local Church is part of being a disciple in our day. Still, certain constraints bind Christianity. For example, individuals may struggle to harmonize the disparities between morality and logic. Or they are pondering whether their discernment is a divine endowment or an inherent human trait.

Sharing in fellowship with other Christians brings a sense of belonging and camaraderie. When things get tough, our faith in God gives us the courage to keep and helps us find the hope to heal. Being with other Christians helps us connect and build lasting relationships with God and other believers.

The Authoritative Book does not mandate the attendance of Saints at Church or critique the doctrines, sermons, and hymns. We should serve the household of God persistently and with dedication regardless of the melodies of merrymaking. The purpose of worship services is to glorify Jehovah, focusing on Him and His greatness. With our hearts full of reverence and appreciation, we express our love and thankfulness to the King of Kings.

Acts 2:42 describes their devotion to teaching, fellowship, breaking bread, and prayer. Today's genuine worship expresses manifold Holy emotions, including enjoyment, grief, conviction, and skepticism.

The author believes the Supreme Being allows the regional Churches to express their adoration freely. Yet, our contemporary interpretation of devotion today might appear strange to the writers of the Sacred Writ. Still, the Almighty has undoubtedly prescribed how He expects the Saints to worship Him through His Word.

The Redeemer takes Holy observance seriously, as seen in the First Chronicle, chapter thirteen. It is why David considered bringing the Visible Ark out of obscurity a top priority 1 Chronicle 13-15. However, the Supreme Being desires the Glorified to praise Him under the banner of Holiness at this age. John 4: 24, "God is Spirit, and His undisputed worshippers respond to Him from their heart."

Churchgoing is an external concept. Our sinful nature resists understanding proven principles. Therefore, we need the physical Body of Christ to sustain us. Doubt, skepticism, and negative thoughts can cause nervousness and uneasiness, leading to bad health. Then a confused believer may see nothing different between Christianity and the secular.

Satan, the author of confusion, is why the Saints cannot make it alone. They must stay in fellowship constantly with other believers. The Glorified needs the strength and prayers of other supporters. But despite the unambiguous nature of the Sacred Writ. Arguments about eschatology prophecy, spiritual gifts, baptism, and Church structure have emerged. But the Bible tells of only one correct interpretation of every Scripture coming from the Word (GOD Breathed).

Yet, even mature, reasonable parish periodically have disagreements. Lucifer realizes that THE LORD'S most potent weapon is a Local Holy flock devoted to Christ, progressively conducting His missions. So, he brings the full speed of evil to prevent and create chaos in the most righteous convocations. But we must remember: "A chain is only as formidable as its weakest link, signifying that a group's power derives from its least capable member."

The Church is an assembly of disciples, made glorious through the grace of God. Though Churchgoers may have different views, the

Bible implores them to serve each other in the Church. Specifically, in Psalm 22: 22, the Writer uses the phrase (brethren) to symbolize the congregation coming together to worship. The great communicator of Hebrew refers to that same passage of Scripture in Hebrews 2: 12, supplanting the expression of "flock" for "gathering." It proves that the perception of the congregation is a loyal crowd of the Author of Salvation.

Gospel teachings on social media can spread the message, but connecting with people of different beliefs is challenging. The brethren are Christ's Bride. Hence, when we forsake the House of God, we are no longer communing with Christ (1 Corinthians 10: 16). By any means, we should Glorify the Almighty. Delightful sounds, pleasing melodies, and praying in the Spirits are uplifting. Christians come together to share their adoration of the Scripture, which gives meaning to their companionship.

So, when the Glorified trust JESUS and His congregation, they can be confident in healing and prosperity results. The Psalmist wrote:

"Shout for joy to THE HOLY ONE, everybody on the earth. Reverence of the Firstborn From the Dead (Rev. 1: 5) with gladness; come before Him with joyful songs. Know that the King of Kings is God. He made us, and we are His; we are His people, the sheep of His pasture. Enter His gates with thanksgiving and His courts with exaltation; thank Him and express admiration for HIS NAME. THE LORD is good, and His love endures forever; His faithfulness continues through every generation" (Psalms 100: 1-5).

Not only does the King of Glory change the heart with His Holy Spirit, but His Word makes us known. When the Saints realize who they are in the Body of Christ, they will unite and learn to accept who they are for their mission. Righteous assurance releases self-doubt. Corporate worship is a time of celebration and enlightenment. The Church gathers to honor the Trinitarian God. So, believers can come together and create a stronger relationship with The Father through assembling.

Everybody wants to know who they are in the Author of Salvation. But, because of television, social media, and the internet, there could be a danger of losing Saint's dedication altogether. The satisfaction of being with fellow Christians, teaching the Bible, and offering a place of fellowship is invaluable. Parishioners must seek spiritual and academic knowledge to participate in Local Church activities.

"The Sacred Writings give you the wisdom that leads to salvation through faith in Christ Jesus. THE LORD inspires every part of Scripture, and so it is profitable for teaching, reproof, correction, and training in righteousness; so that the individual of Jehovah may be adequate, equipped for all excellent work." 2 Timothy 3:15-17.

So, when the Community Congregation disengages from Christian Education, it poses a threat of not having an accord with JESUS. The Glorified separation causes them to commit to the wrong thing, making life worse instead of better. The Church must show that physical worship actively engages with sermons, classes, and asking questions.

For instance, "Autodidact" means self-taught. Separation from Church teachings leaves one exposed to Satan's attacks. Down the line, the stress of unacceptance by other Saints develops into a terror. And the fear of someone uncovering our identity and the inner turmoil of fearing people knowing we are not as perfect as we want them to believe. Severing ties with Christ-centered supporters created a deep void, growing larger and swallowing up all feelings of joy.

Therefore, a break from the Church may cause alarm and stop followers from protecting themselves from wickedness. Unrighteousness is often associated with loneliness and discomfort. When not habitually engaging in Church activities, it's an uncomfortable feeling.

THE FIRSTBORN OVER Creation makes the case that human discomfort stems from a heart of unbelief. These are those who doubt the power of the Bride of Christ. The plausibility structure does not accommodate the Gospel, making it unacceptable. The Bible speaks to faith as confidence, hope, and trust that the Lord is at work, even though it is not always visible. Faith understands that the Lord is actively involved, whether ours or someone else's. For example, Jesus gently rebukes His disciples for their lack of faultless insight to pray together, "O you of little faith" (Matthew 8: 26).

So, we must trust our local Churches regardless of their abundant imperfections. Besides, The Word shows fellowshiping helps calm and enhances the effects of righteous therapy. The Sacred Scripture instructs us to dedicate ourselves to the Apostles' teaching, fellowship, and communion (Acts 2: 42).

Reverencing God's Holiness and sharing faith amongst nonbelievers is remarkable. Working together constructively leads to unity in the House of Prayer. But defining Godly goodness according to human wisdom will lead to mistrust, shame, and blame-shifting (see Genesis 3:1-13). Divine wisdom gives us peace, understanding, and the power to decide and make choices with assurance and clarity.

But the burden of anti-intellectualism has been a constant thread winding its way through the evangelic Church. A group of happy-medium so-called Christians ignorantly undermines the Gospel with profit evangelism. They claim teaching the Sacred Text is a get-rich-quick scheme the Saints can use for their well-being. Prosperous preaching has overwhelmed Churches nationwide, suffocating believers' faith and leading them astray. Prosperity theology by the false notion that "their ignorance is just as good as God's Christian Doctrine."

But the Bible is not a personal Letter addressed to a single individual. When someone quotes the Divine Writ out of context, the hearers receive an incorrect message. By removing the word "we" and using "me," we can mistakenly believe that the Gospel is only relevant to ourselves and our ideas about Christianity.

THE LORD did not inspire the writers to write the Scripture to personal anybody; it is a Holy Document inscribed to every human. So, Doctrine, as outlined in Scripture, is the full suite of essential theological truths that make up God's message, laid out in 1 Timothy 1: 10. Pedagogy theory regards the Hallowed Handbook as a crucial source of counsel for humanity.

The Word of God's interpretation is for the entire Body of Christ. Scripture guides us in living out our faith. Especially, Biblical expository teaching is preaching that reveals the depth and breadth of the Scripture. But lack of trust attacks the Lion of the Tribe of Judah as a myth, equal to Santa Claus, when The Hope of Glory does not meet their needs.

Instead, they blame THE AUTHOR of Creation for having a ludicrous idea that they should have abandoned when they grew up intellectually. But disempowered beliefs mean the GREAT SHEPHERD is not their EVERYTHING. Doubt inhibits one's confidence in the Father. He is not the supplier of their life. Then they only seek THE LORD as an emergency source, saying, ("The only thing left for me to do now is to pray"). But prayer should have been the first obligation!

Finally, we will answer the question. What is Church Affiliation, and how is it relevant today? It is a joint effort of Saints combining forces to serve the Lord and declare his house His Own. Saintly admiration, loyalty, belief, and deference distinguish Scripture. So, Christ's Supernatural Body, the Church, is an outward display of His Divine greatness, made up of a multitude of devoted followers. And it symbolizes His existence around the world. The Church building incorporates the correct elements representing the Living Body of Jesus Christ.

So, we should unite with a Local Chapel because the Firstborn Over All Creation loves His Christian organization and offers Himself for it.

If you delight yourself in the Author of Life, you must be intimate with His Temple and devoted to it. The Holy Writ commands, "Husbands, love your wives, just as Christ also cherished the Place of Worship and gave His Precious Blood for it." Ephesians 5: 25.

Nicky Gumbel said: "Church is not an organization you join; it is a family where you belong, a home where they love you, and a hospital where you find healing."[1]

CHAPTER 15

THE NUTS AND BOLTS OF CHRISTIANITY

Unlike pagan religions, God originated Christianity. Ephesians 1: 4 says: "Even as He chose us in Him before the foundation of the world to be Holy." By acknowledging that Christ's work on the cross leads to righteousness, Christians can show their ethical loyalty to the church. So, the Saints can be confident in their salvation. Still, we sometimes get involved in intense and enthusiastic conflicts.

Paul asked: "Is Christ divided?" 1 Corinthians 1:12-13. His statement per se is not condemning denominations. Christians have disagreed on tradition and theological issues since the founding of Christianity. Nevertheless, they have consistently joined forces to assist each other under the banner of morality. Unity allows them to study, increase their power, and show the planet exactly Who the Ultimate Authority is.

Paul wrote to the Church in Rome: "Each of us has one body with many members. And these members do not have the same purpose, so in Christ, we though differently in form one body, and each member belongs to the others. We have unique gifts according to the grace given to each of us. The Holy Spirit has gifted each believer, especially for the good of the Body of Christ. Specifically, if your gift is prophesying, prophesy according to your faith." Romans 12: 4-6.

One Saint had the ability of assurance. Another had the power to heal, a third the capability to perform miracles, and yet another the discernment of spirits. First Corinthians chapter 12. So, let us answer the question. How do you know what your gift is? Fair question! The writer has sixty-plus years of salvation and prays constantly, but Jocephus is not an intercessor. These righteous mediators can stay on their knees for hours in prayer. Specifically, what we find easy to do while others may grapple with is your gift, my friend.

So, the Supreme Being has given every believer a gift, enabling them to fulfill His vision of righteousness. And to uphold "the customary good" of the Body of Christ (1 Corinthians 12: 7) and to build up the Church (1 Corinthians 14:12). Exercising this gift will give the Saint righteous fulfillment, purpose, and contentment in their work. One's inborn abilities will lead them to success in life. That means one will focus on their strengths and develop them instead of excessively complaining.

Supporters favored by God's Nature give them the abilities, skills, and proficiency that decide what they can do. Specifically, it encompasses the tangible evidence that the righteous have the approval of THE LORD. God's grace gives the Glorified the ability to do something humanly impossible. When we prefer someone, we want to be with them and delight in that person.

As proof, the Author and Perfecter of our Faith have faith in His Saints since He knows them well; since the dawn of time, He wanted to commune with us. He created humankind in His Image. Genesis 1: 26-28. 'Let us make man in our image, according to our likeness, and let them rule over the fish of the sea and the birds of the sky, the cattle, and the entire earth.'

In "The Nuts and Bolts of Christianity," the critical elements of the necessity of Holiness. Salvation is by God's grace and not by works; it is redemption through Jesus Christ alone. Ephesians 2: 8-9.

The Glorified tells the world that the Redeemer loves them with immense love and desires to save them from their sins. So, "In your hearts honor Christ the Lord as holy, always being prepared to defend anyone who asks you for a reason for the hope in you; yet do it with gentleness and respect." 1 Peter 3: 15.

Despite this, non-believers of Christianity regard the disciples of Jesus as deceitful. Because of their proclaimed piety, their deeds do not match their words. But the most efficient way to share one's faith is to live a Godly life. Someone said, "Integrity is doing the right thing, even when no one is watching." The faithful should be receptive and candid with others regarding our experiences with THE LORD. Then cease fretting over, making them another salvation appendage. "One planted, another watered, but the Deity gives the increase." 1 Corinthians 3: 6-8.

Further, the Nuts and Bolts of Christianity include the specific vocation of calling those who are dead in sin to a life of eternal righteousness. Millions in the free world do not see Easter as a celebration of the resurrection of Jesus. Undoubtedly, it pains the Chief Shepherd to know that hundreds of thousands in the United States of America have not heard the Gospel.

Primitive emotions stop the Saints from sharing the Sacred Text. So, too, impending threats, evil, and agony, whether real or imagined. Yet, without hearing the Gospel, there is no ordinary means of deliverance from the immoral and wickedness; more often, our free will allows us to choose.

It is simultaneously true for the Local Church—Jesus' command to share the Gospel is an example. He gave us the vision to tell every nation re His redemption, and as His followers, we should make sharing Righteous Doctrine Credibility our aim. Christians, however, are not working to fulfill the "Great Commission" Matthew 28: 18-20—at least not enthusiastically with purpose. So, too often, our soul-winning goals collapse because we place restrictions upon ourselves. Often, what holds us back are the human extremities we place upon ourselves.

Human trepidation is a Saint reacting negatively toward the Author of Life's message. Again, fear is the most significant circumference in limiting Gospel sharing. For instance, if evangelizing means traveling outside our comfort zone, worry may stop us. But if we stay in a particular location or have us minister to familiar people, we willingly serve.

But we should identify the obstacles standing in our way and pray for forgiveness. Strengthen your faith by praying, reading the Bible, and sharing the good news of salvation with everyone. Yet countless believers prioritize their comfort over exploring the Word. Traditional spiritual beliefs do not connect with modern life and service. We must study to show ourselves approved.

Thus, what was for Christians in the past could be foreign to most youthful adults. THE LORD inspired humans to publish the Bible in 1611; so, over four hundred years, it has had a heartfelt effect on humankind. Still, the HOLY BOOK is from ages ago; thus, we must be relevant today. Suppose the Glorified continues the trajectory of transmitting folk tales. Church erosion will increase significantly, putting the devoted at risk of becoming an extension of broken faith.

The Bible's matchless message—redemption—universally and perpetually applies to humanity. God's Word will never be outdated, superseded, or improved upon by society. Cultures change, and laws vary. People will misinterpret Jehovah's Word, but that does not mean it has changed.

The Gospel offers assurance for anyone who strayed from their faith in THE LORD. But the Saints who do not heed the warning against desiring to hear what they want to hear; (2 Timothy 4: 3-4 is a must-read for them). If they continue down the path of grab and blab, they will have little regard for God's Word. Then they accept a notion based on someone's faith and thus become deceived into their proclamation. Psalm 107 details finding their path back to the Author and Perfecter of our faith.

For example, when a believer experiences loss, they come to THE GREAT HIGH PRIEST with a broken heart after they hear a sermon or teaching that moved them. Thus, they have confidence in the Holy One and proclaim their faith in their fleeing ardor. However, they no longer trust the Blessed and Sole Ruler, Christ, as time passes to keep them happy and safe.

Besides, their strong faith has shifted to human weakness. Hence, they say suddenly, without careful consideration: "Here is what I am doing to support my deliverance." But humankind's effort, unaccompanied by The Creator's sacrificial death and resurrection, cannot forgive sins. As an old hymn declares, "What can wash away my sin? Nothing but the blood of JESUS."

Besides, Matthew 7: 21-23, THE HOLY AND TRUE warns us, "Not everyone who calls out to ME, 'LORD! LORD!' will enter the Kingdom of Paradise—only those who DO THE BIDDING OF MY FATHER IN HEAVEN. On Judgment Day, COUNTLESS may say JESUS, 'THE SON of GOD! We PROPHESIED (or PREACHED), CAST OUT DEMONS, and PERFORMED MIRACLES IN YOUR NAME.' But I SHALL reply, 'I never knew you. Get away from Me, you who BREAK MY FATHER'S LAWS."

Those familiar with the Bible comprehend the current denials of Christianity. Despite attempts to stop the Word! Showing the power of Jesus Christ, His resolute followers oppose frivolous disbelief and polytheism. Although, the Saints must continue to answer meaningful questions:

1. What is salvation
2. What takes place in the human spirit after death

3. Does God rule? Then why does He tolerate evil
4. Is speaking in tongues a gift

Self-Bible Study is a significant first step in answering and growing for new and mature believers. Autonomous enlightenment increases faith by drawing closer to God through prayer and examining His Word. Avoiding the above questions can worsen things for the universal and local congregations. The author will give a concise answer to the inquiries above bullet points. Then motivate the readers to do an in-depth research investigation after each topic.

CHAPTER 16

WHAT IS SALVATION?

Before the writer can talk about salvation, we must understand why anybody needs it.

(1) Holy preservation. Without sustaining guardianship from the Holy Spirit, one cannot know God or His Kingdom.

(2) It would be challenging to understand the teachings of the Bible. But after an individual gives their life to Christ, their eyes are open to the truth of His Word. The Lord Jesus Christ, "I give them eternal life, and they shall never perish; no one can snatch them from my hand. My Father, who has given them to me, is greater than all; no one can take them from My Begetter's firm grasp" (John 10: 28-29).

(3) In (Ephesians 4:30), the Apostle Paul explains those who yield to the Faithful and True Witness (Revelation 3:14), the Father, will seal for the day of redemption. So, "Impossible for a spiritually dead person to know THE LORD and trust in His Word. One must ask Jesus to deliver from a sinful life to live as the Almighty intended. Following righteousness is the key to living a purposeful and free life through divine redemption.

So, from the foundation of the world, The Deity created humankind to have a perfect relationship with Him (Genesis 1: 26). Further, the Book of Genesis shows THE LORD made an ideal world for humankind's first parents. But they wrecked their relationship and home with Jehovah when they rebelled against the Almighty by eating from the forbidden tree. They did not attain knowledge as Satan promised, but rejected God's will in their thoughtless favor (Genesis 3:1–13). Because of their disobedience, Adam and Eve received dire consequences. Read Genesis chapter Three.

The First Parents' rebelliousness was devastating, bringing sin and death into the world. But what is exceptional is that God gave His Son to save humanity, seeing that humans cannot rescue themselves from eternal death. Jesus is the promised Messiah Who came to the earth to save sinners (Luke 19: 10). Given that every human comes into the world with Adam and Eve's sins (Romans 3: 23). No human could ever pay the penalty of their sins (in the past, present, and future) with our labors constrained and insufficient.

Too, behaving differently, giving money to worthy causes, or a life full of moral behavior cannot save from sin. Receive salvation from sin by having faith in Jesus Christ, repenting, and baptism. Hebrews chapter Four tells us that Jesus has made a new and living way for us to come before God based on His Sacrificial Blood.

The Author of Life's crucifixion made it possible to stand before the Father without having our sins counted against us. Instead, we stand dressed in Jesus' righteousness. We no longer must fear the sting of death. Through the crucifixion, Jesus has conquered it forever. His death was a brutal and horrific embitterment that cost Him temporary access to God the Father. And yet He did it willingly to show every human the infinite reach of righteous love to defeat death and prove His Kingdom.

Recovering from undesirable evildoings allows us to appreciate righteousness over evil. The Supreme Being's preservation is the most significant expression of His love for humankind. Thus, salvation means Christ, THE LORD rescues us from unrighteousness's consequences. But lack of reverence for God and His truth causes one to suffer the consequences of oppression. Then, they usually impose their cruelty on someone else.

It takes discernment to adhere to God's moral law. But doing wrong pertains to an act that does not adhere to Biblical justice and integrity. Having salvation means to rise above sin's restrictions.

So, THE LORD'S redemption is the rescue of the soul counter to transgression and the consequences of immoralities. It is the pursuit of saving a person from sin. The Apostle Paul said the payment for sin (is death) in Romans 6: 23. Jesus' death brings a person to the Father through the Holy Spirit. Because of the Son of God's execution, burial, and resurrection, humans can request forgiveness for their sins. Hence, the process of atonement continues eternally (Romans 6: 23).

Christians and sinners understand the value of avoiding sin for everlasting life. But unlike trespassers, God transports the Glorified from the eternal hellfire in readiness for the devil, and his angels (Matthew 25: 41). The punishment for sin is an infinite discipline in the Lake of Fire for the unredeemed. However, by accepting the Gospel, wrongdoers liberate themselves from the terrible destiny of their sins.

1 John 1: 9 tells the readers, "If we confess our misconduct, he is faithful and just, and will forgive one's faults and purify them from every unrighteousness."

Jesus' atonement freed us from the eternal pain of death. Redemption for the entire human race comes to them by faith only in the Nazarene. He is the Liberator for humanity, opposing sin and its consequence of everlasting retribution of a Divine plan to save humans.

He is the Heir of Every-Thing (Hebrew 1: 2) and lifts the Glorified to a unique spiritual body, justified by God (Romans 6: 4). The different life is possible because Jesus died for the sinner's sins and then rose from the dead (three days later). So, because of His resurrection, repentant believers carry the power to rule and reign in this world. They no longer need to stay hopeless. Even though moral development will prove manifold challenges, the Horn of Salvation is the Saint's safeguard. Since we now belong to Christ, we can take possession of Hope in Him.

But more, we die spiritually in Him and rise with Him in eternity! Acknowledging JESUS's sacrificial death helps one choose righteousness over wrongdoing. Only the Saints achieve sovereignty over immoral acts because the Redeemer gave His Life for humanity. Specifically, the King of kings was the "sin-bearer." And when they murdered Him on the cross, the Law of unrighteousness ceased to gain power over His supporters. These are the details of atonement.

The Biblical Text sometimes means achievement, health, or preservation. But always liberation from unethical behavior and its consequences. Salvation lifts life's uncertainties. Thus, restitution, too, carries a physical proclamation, such as Paul's freedom from confinement. For example, Paul was in prison, but his righteousness never allowed the jail cell to overwhelm his spirit (Philippians 1: 19).

Redemption has a timeless, Spiritual connotation. The jailer in Philippi asked the Apostle. "What must he do to be saved," referring to the jailer's unyielding destiny (Acts 16: 30-31). The incredible tremor and Paul's eagerness for the Gospel gave him the confidence to lead the jailer to salvation.

God's preserving gracefulness is better and more comprehensive than one may think. His favor not only grants absolution but also reinstates justice and absolves those guilty of committing a grave sin. Godliness and kindness reconcile and reaffirm faith to propitiate to purify. The sovereign compassionateness of God saves humans from their sins.

The Lamb Without Blemish leads us to consider His Biblical Doctrine makes up the details of sanctification.

SELF-STUDY SALVATION SCRIPTURE:

"Titus 3: 5, Romans 10: 9, Acts 4: 12, Ephesians 2: 8, John 14: 6, 1 John 1: 9, 1 John 5: 13, 1 Peter 2: 24, 1 Peter 3: 21, 1 Thessalonians 5: 9, 2 Corinthians 5: 17, 2 Corinthians 5: 21, 2 Corinthians 6: 2, 2 Peter 3: 9, 2 Thessalonians 2: 13, 2 Timothy 1: 9, Acts 11: 18, Acts 16: 31,"

"Acts 2: 38, Acts 22: 16, Acts 28: 28, Ephesians 1: 13, Ephesians 2: 10, Galatians 2: 21, James 2: 18, John 1: 12, John 3: 16, John 3: 3, John 3: 36, John 3: 5, John 5: 24, John 6: 37, John 6: 44, Jonah 2: 9, Mark 16: 16, Matthew 7: 21, Philippians 1: 6, Philippians 2: 12, Psalm 25: 5, Psalm,"

"Romans 1: 16, Romans 10: 13, Font 3: 23, Font 5: 8, Font 6: 14, Font 6: 23." The list is not exhaustive.

CHAPTER 17

WHAT OCCURS IN THE HUMAN SPIRIT AFTER DEATH?

HOW NON-CHRISTIANS AND CHRISTIANS VIEW DEATH

Death is a source of panic for all humans. It's the demise of the permanent stopping of all vital bodily activities, concluding life and presence. Dying ends humankind's earthly life and all they enjoy. Historically, science has held death as a termination of the lifecycle.

Doctors prefer brain functioning or no blood going to the brain as a definition of death over the silent of a heart beating. But mortality is not the end, according to faith-based believers. (God speaking through the Prophet, says, "Before I formed you in the womb, I knew you." Jeremiah 1: 5). Life results from the soul or the spirit. When the soul departs from the body, physical life expires.

The continuation of earthly life depends on conserving the body's health. It is reasonable to ask what happens to the soul after death. Hinduism and Buddhism, for instance, argue the body is a husk, and the spirit makes the individual unique. However, skilled researchers believe a heart takes residence in the body for around 21 or 22 days when life begins.

Christianity differs from other religions in its view of death.

While the Holy Bible is the basis of Christianity, 2 Timothy 3: 16-17. The Quran justifies the Muslim faith, revealed by the angel Gabriel to the Prophet Muhammad. And the entire Bible, the Almighty, inspired by its efficacy to enlighten humankind on what is right and make them aware of what is wrong in their lives. So, it corrects the Saints when they are wrong and teaches them to do what is right.

And so, Islam honors Jesus as God's messenger; they call Him a 'Muslim' because of His moral teachings. However, Christians know the Almighty as Jehovah Jara, which means "God provides" and the Savior of Humanity. The Bible suggests that the Glorified should not be selfish or seek validation from others. Christ is the only Individual who can provide supporters with what we require—in body, soul, and spirit. When we lose our trust in the Chief Shepherd, we entrust our belief in The Hope of Glory, who comprehends and cherishes us deeply.

Muslims maintain humans are born innocent and must abide by the Law of God. Hinduism claims there are multiple divinities. Buddhism revolves around Buddha's awakening, and agony results from human craving.

However, to keep this writing short, as I promise, all these leading religions concur that the spirit migrates to another realm after it has vacated the body. Opposed to other beliefs, Buddhism does not acknowledge an eternal supernatural essence of the human identity. Specifically, they argue humans are without an immortal soul. But the Saints believe God took Jesus to Paradise to live with Him after His resurrection. Therefore, Christians also believe our souls will go to Heaven when we die.

Christianity believes in the crucifixion of Jesus Christ. They profess Jesus Christ as God's progeny and humanity's rescuer. As Christians believe the Bible to be the word of God, they look to this source to grasp what awaits them after death and in the afterlife. Despite differences of opinion, Christians remain unified. Christians believe those who accept Jesus Christ as their Lord and Savior will ascend to Heaven after death. Different denominations have differing beliefs on the immediacy of going to Heaven after death.

Despite a widespread Christian conviction that souls will ascend to Heaven upon death, the Bible also outlines a day of resurrection. The day of judgment will come when Jesus returns to Earth. This resurrection of Christ is in (1 Thessalonians 4), which says:

"Brothers and sisters, we do not want you to be uninformed about those who sleep in death so that you do not grieve like the rest of humankind, who have no hope. For we believe Jesus died and rose again, and so we believe God will bring with Jesus those who have fallen asleep in him. According to the Lord's word, we tell you we who are still alive, left until the coming of the Lord, will certainly not precede those who have fallen asleep. The ALMIGHTY will descend from Heaven with a powerful command, accompanied by the voice of the archangel and the trumpet blast of God. THE LORD will resurrect those who have died in His Son. After that, we who are still alive and left will catch up with them in the clouds to meet the Lord in the air. And so, we will be with the Lord forever."

Habitually, uncertainty exists in the Christian faith regarding post-mortem conditions. It is a widespread belief that God judges sinners and sends them to their eternal destination upon death. Multifarious believe that after death, everyone "sleeps" until the final judgment, after which we go to Heaven or the underworld. Conversely, others suggest their souls and spirits go to purgatory, a temporary expiatory for purification upon death. While there, they await their final resurrection, judgment, and eternal destination.

So, what does the Bible say happens after death?

It's natural to contemplate what follows life. Again, physically, death is when the body's vital organs, including the lungs, heart, and brain, are no longer functioning. Upon death, the spirit persists. Upon our demise, our spirit transcends our physical form and journeys to the spiritual realm in anticipation of resurrection. The Spirit World had two partitioned realms: Heaven and Hades.

Christians have no cause to fear death. The Bible emphatically states that when the Saints expire, they go straightaway to be with Christ. Thus, they are safe in the Father's grasp when they pass from this earthly life. And nothing "In the universe, will sever them from the affection of God that is in Christ Jesus our THE LORD" (Romans 8: 39).

Christian's going to Heaven exulted entry is in multiple verses of the Bible. Jesus said, "He is the resurrection and the life. "Those who trust in Him will have life, even though they die" (John 11: 25). Paul wanted to unite with Christ (Philippians 1: 23). 2 Corinthians 5:1 states we have an everlasting home in Heaven.

Jesus will give us new figures comparable to His Body after His resurrection. They will be invulnerable to any ailment or agony and not age. However, we must remember one extra truth: God will reunite our spirits and bodily forms after this present age.

Thus, a Christian's passing differs from the unrighteous' unfortunate demise. They see death not as an adversary and the end of life but as a companion and the start of something new for the Saints. Although death is inevitable for Christians, they do not possess everlasting life during their lifetime. THE LORD praises the faithful laborer. Come, rest on my palace's porch. Now is the time to enter and experience the joy of Christ for what He offers after leaving the earth.

Again, Christians do not believe in conceptualizing reincarnation or second chances. They understand the Firstborn from the Dead (Romans 6: 23) is the Son of God, and He guides a disciple's spirit to

Him after they die. The study of God's Word unlocks the mysteries of the Christian's ever-abiding awareness following the end of life. So, the reward is unceasing joyfulness for those living by the Presbyterianism Doctrine.

For instance, the Bible tells us precisely what happens to the spirit, heart, and anatomy after death. The physical framework ceases to exist. To save one's soul from eternal damnation, one must confess wrongdoing to the Redeemer and have faith in the Lord (1 John 2:2).

The Head of the Church (Ephesians 1: 22; 4: 15; 5: 23) died on the cross for humanity's liberation, saving them from endless imprisonment. But the Father raised Him from the dead to show His supporters He is The Hope of Glory, and they have victory over death. Now, the Son of Jehovah Is the only Name under Heaven deliverance from the act of evil exists." Acts 4: 12.

So, the Biblical Text is the most comprehensive Gospel presentation explaining the departed. It teaches the redeemed and unredeemed to manage their actions. That tells us the righteous will possess the earth, and they shall live forever on it, Psalm 37: 29. Afresh, after an unsaved person dies, they go to a region called the underworld, or Hades, a prison for the dead.

Once more, the Bible also calls it Sheol or Torments. These people did not accept THE LORD while living on earth. See Luke Chapter 16. But the "crown of glory" (1 Peter 5: 4) given through faith in the Blessed and only Ruler to all who believe while we are conscious. Jesus, the Resurrection, and Life said:

"He is the Supreme Being of Abraham, Isaac, and Jacob." Immanuel (Matthew 1: 23) is not the Savior of the dead, but the living" (Luke 20: 38). The interpretation: everybody in Christ is alive and endures throughout eternity. But their physical anatomy is still bound to go to the grave.

The innate spirit detaches from the torso and continues to Jesus until Judgment Day (2 Corinthians 5: 1-8). So, no matter what we achieve, it will be frivolous because the human body will someday turn to dust. Thus, nobody can prevent their body's return to the earth and extinction. The writer's statement is not a license to give up on your dreams and vision. The Bible encourages us to seek a career. Besides, If anyone is unwilling to work, let him not eat (2 Thessalonians 3: 10).

The Alpha and Omega endowed Solomon with the knowledge to record: "The dust shall revert to the dust," which explains the body's dissolution process. The interpretation is that dirt settles and retreats to grime, but "the inner being will return to the Deity who gave it" (Ecclesiastes 12: 7). So, for people living outside of Christ, their spirit goes to a spiritual realm of suffering. "The one who rejects Me and does not receive my words has a judge; the word that I have spoken, they are bound to condemn them on the last day." John 12: 48.

The author's statement is not a scary tactic. Humans that decide evil over grace move to a permanent home of mourners after departing from life. But we who are in THE LORD will spend eternity with THE SAVIOR, contingent on one's choice of Him, before dying. So, choose the Messiah or die in infernal regions.

Those who reject JESUS, the Source of Salvation, condemn themselves like murderers after death. So, human justice calls for a more sizeable punishment on an indistinguishable footing. Thus, the righteous must do all they can to share their indestructible faith with them to keep them from dying in their misdoing. Apart from Christ, infinite suffering is imminent. Yet, everyone has an equal chance of perpetual immortality after making Immanuel, The Hope of Glory, their Savior.

But the contrast between human mistakes for Christians does not remove everlasting grace; the author's statement is not a license to wrongdoing. He shows immortal existence is a world of freedom, comfort, strength, and confidence. But the unsaved have a different destination from eternal living altogether. Their aftermath of not accepting the Creator's salvation causes them to spend eternity in the abyss.

They are fleeing to perish in their insurrection and have no faith. As Jesus in John 3: 36 cautioned, "God's wrath remains on the unredeemed." Hence, grace neutralizes nobody's wrong decisions. Still, nobody could misbehave more than Jehovah's favor can cover if they accept the Head of the Church as Savior.

So, the believer who sows unhealthy seeds will expect a mediocre harvest in this life and the afterlife. The Supreme Being alone has the Authority to pay off the penalty for our sins. Repentance has overtones of righteousness for the Saints and others that attract the attention of the Almighty. Christians who have lived in ungodliness know how disheartening it can be. Yet, even after their moral disgrace, THE HOLY ONE still cares for them. But they must repent if they want to receive God's forgiveness.

THE LORD shows salvation and freedom when an individual is a kingdom citizen. For example, JESUS denounced the cities; He performed miracles with weak faith. "Woe to you, Chorazin! "Trouble to you, Bethsaida! The supernatural phenomenon you saw Me do, had Tyre and Sidon seen, they may have repented in sackcloth and ashes. But I tell you, it will be more bearable for them on the day of judgment than for you because you did not repent your sins." Matthew 11: 20-22.

The Old Testament Book of Psalms speaks of the deceased's dwelling beneath the earth, waiting for the ultimate test of humanity, known as Sheol or Hades. Inferno's "second death" is an unpleasant experience that involves constant pain, agony, and sensory torture.

For example, in the story of Lazarus, the beggar, and the affluent potentate captain, Luke 16: 19-31 tells of a Great Gulf separating paradise from the location of torment. The vagabond tramp was at the heart of Abraham enjoying himself, and the prosperous gentleman was suffering in Sheol. Not because he was wealthy, but what he counted on when he was alive in the body, namely his wealth. Nor did the panhandler man enjoy Abraham's bosom because he was poor. Regardless of the lack of knowledge about money, this derelict individual trusted the Almighty.

Without the Good Shepherd as the SAVIOR, the unsaved souls shall go to eternal damnation after Christians and sinners' Day of segregation. But the faithful Glorified will continue to the perpetual Heaven following a 1,000-year dynasty of Emmanuel on earth. The Millennium reign of God the Son is in Revelation chapter 20. Too, see Things to Come: A Study in Biblical Eschatology by J. Dwight Pentecost.

After Death Scripture

John 11: 25, John 5: 24, John 3: 16, Luke 23: 43, Romans 6: 23, 1 Corinthians 15: 26, 1 Thessalonians 4: 13, 2 Corinthians 5: 8, Acts 24: 15, Daniel 12: 2, Ecclesiastes 12: 7, Ecclesiastes 9: 5, Genesis 3: 19, Hebrews 9: 27, John 14: 6, John 16: 22, Luke 16: 23, Matthew 10: 28, Matthew 25: 41, Matthew 25: 46, Matthew 27: 52, Philippians 1: 21, Proverbs 12: 28, Psalm 116: 15, Psalm 146: 4, Revelation 1: 18, Revelation 14: 13, Revelation 21: 4, Revelation 21: 8, Romans 14: 8.

CHAPTER 18

GOD RULES

Even though it's daunting to talk to non-believers, God takes on the mistakes of His faithful followers who believe in His Son. And how THE LORD imposed the penalty on (Jesus), The Hope of Glory, as if He had done humankind's transgressions.

The Scripture reveals that God will resurrect His people upon the return of Jesus Christ and reign with Him on the earth. Christ was never under the control of sin, so His death was unrelated to His falling from grace. Nonetheless, He was charged with our sins. Yet, Jesus' death on the cross signified the conclusion of the Law's power over humanity. This implies that for Christians, death is an unconscious provisional state.

The Author of Life's death was necessary for those lost to understand the consequences of rejecting Jesus' salvation. Despite this, it is still hard to empathize with those who have experienced immense suffering from the wickedness of others. Yet, we can take comfort in the Almighty's assurance that one day, evil will no longer exist.

The Hope of Glory King Eternal said about evil: "I will bring you to a horrible end, and you will be no more...declares THE SOVEREIGN LORD." Ezekiel 26: 21

Despite evil, the Apostle Peter encourages, "With God's mercy, He heals, confirms, and stabilizes. So, may he have dominion over everything for all eternity. And let amen be the sum of our prayers." 1 Peter 5: 10-11

Still, why the Supreme Being tolerates evil is a puzzle that has confounded individuals for generations. People theorize: The LORD works through sin to free souls. But responses to this query depend much on one's faith and worldview. The Faithful and True Witness sovereign rule allows iniquity, allowing people to discern right from wrong. But others believe evil aids in spiritual growth.

It is essential to remember one's religious stance on evil; THE LORD is constant in our lives, even in times of pain and wickedness. Psalms 96: 4 conveys that no deity is absolute to The Man from Heaven. In contrast to Our Sacrificed Passover Lamb, Satan is powerless. The above verse implies that THE LORD should be in awe and trepidation above all other deities. The Beginning and End will direct Satan and his fellow angels to the underworld. Besides, the Atoning Sacrifice for our Sins created Satan, Who Originated everything.

The Father is a benevolent Messiah who cares profoundly for those who trust in the Great High Priest to seek solace and wisdom from Him. Hence, we can know God's "perfect will" when we read and obey Romans 12: 2:

Resist the temptation to accept the way of the world. But go through a conversion of your mentality. Openness to the Almighty's will leads to a perfect and complete plan, regardless of evil. Thus, you can discern and concur with the Blessed and only Ruler what is helpful, pleasing, and blameless (study Romans Chapter 12).

As the Author of Life is All-Knowing, He knows what He will bring to pass within us. His infallible design considers our lack of understanding, vulnerability, sins, and even the sins of others inflicted upon us (Genesis 50: 20). "For I know the plans I have for you," declares THE LORD, "plans to prosper you and not to harm you, plans to give you hope and a future," Jeremiah 29: 11. So, His plan and purpose for every believer are for their excellent, and His Glory (see Romans 8: 28). Which includes suffering and tragedy that comes to us in life (see 2 Corinthians 1: 3-7; 12: 7-10).

Salvation liberates us from the domination of sin. Without redemption, we may always fall victim to corruption and embrace its authority (see Romans 6: 20–23, 7: 14–15). If an individual is in bondage to wickedness, they cannot please Jehovah (Romans 8: 8). Despite our abundant attempts to start over, visit the Church, and do virtuous deeds. But apart from Christ, the spirit is wicked, and we face God's justice.

Salvation expresses the ALL-POWERFUL LOVE. Again, by taking the punishment for our sins on the cross, Jesus enabled us to receive the blessing of release from our sins. Through the benevolence of Holiness, referenced in 1 John 1:9. Christ Jesus (JEHOVAH) purifies us of every unrighteousness.

Jesus exemplified overcoming evil with good; "No revenge. The Author and Perfecter of our Faith placed his hope in the righteous Judge. By submitting to His captors, He triumphed over sin, Satan, and death (Ephesians 4: 8–10). The day of the crucifixion was a victory for redemption. Through surrendering to the Father's powerful will, Jesus overcame sin with good.

CHAPTER 19

IS SPEAKING IN TONGUES A GIFT

The short answer is yes. The Bible recorded the first occurrence of speaking in tongues in Acts 2:1-4. Approximately 120 followers of Jesus Christ had assembled in an Upper Room on the Day of Pentecost. Despite their single language, the Holy Spirit enabled the apostles to spread the Gospel in multiple dialects. When believers today discuss speaking in tongues, sundry disputes and enigmatic queries appear. For instance:

- Is this contemporary-day glossolalia (or speaking in tongues) the original thing? To any extent, the Saint's claim to be tongues today is fraudulent, unlike those performed in Scripture. No matter how profoundly one presents them or how significant they may appear. The most legitimate use of tongues originates in Acts chapter 2, Acts chapter 10, and Acts chapter 19: 6.

- Today's tongues, are they from God? Yes, in episodes in the Bible, individuals baptized in the Holy Spirit spoke in tongues. Sometimes at that exact moment, see Acts Chapter One and Chapter 19: 5-7.

- Are they for the Church of today? Speaking in tongues saves nobody. And they are not a sign of the Holy Spirit in you. So, Christian denominations claim that speaking in tongues is not for today's Church but ended with the early Church. Still, the Apostle Paul said to the first Church years after JESUS' crucifixion. "So, my siblings, be eager to prophesy and do not forbid speaking in tongues (1 Corinthians 14: 39).

- Are they for every Christian? "The promise is to you and your children, and to everyone THE LORD OUR GOD shall call." Acts 2: 39-KJV. Thus, they contend that speaking in tongues is not for every believer. 1 Corinthians proved this contention erroneous 14: 27. "The Saint speaking in an unknown tongue, let one interpret." (1 Corinthians 14: 27)

Sincere people have often claimed to experience speaking in tongues. Should we doubt their expression of spirituality? Are they misled and misguided, relevant to the gift of tongues? Christians must use spiritual discernment when analyzing Biblical teachings on speaking in tongues. If their claims are false, we must educate them through Christian Doctrine.

The Bible methodically construes as the apostles shared the Good News of righteousness to various ethnicities. Each monoglot heard the message in their language and said, "We hear them declaring the wonders of God in our tongues!" Acts 2: 11. Astounding the Greek Word translates tongues as "vocabularies." The gift of tongues specifies the speaker speaking the Gospel not known to an individual but understanding it in their dialect.

Yet, here is the unfavorable rub; in 1 Corinthians chapters 12–14, Paul discusses the phenomenal use of the gifts of tongues. "Now, brothers, if I come to you speaking in tongues, what good it can be to you unless it brings you revelation or knowledge" (1 Corinthians 14: 6). So, speaking in tongues is valuable to the one speaking. But, useless to everyone unless someone interprets them. Acts chapter Two tells not the aural faculty of an individual language but the auditory perception of a heavenly message in one's sense of hearing. Can this phenomenon still occur today? It can, but rarely is a translator present, making the speaker highly suspicious.

In Chapter Twelve, Paul lists seven spiritual gifts and asks if everyone has them. Does everyone speak in tongues? Is each person an interpreter?" The obvious answer to the seven instances is an obvious "No."

Christians who speak in tongues have no individual standing over non-speakers. A Saint or denomination concentrates on the languages spoken. Still, they believe they are more mature Christians and have a rapprochement with the Holy Spirit. They will miss the most significant piece of Christianity: witnessing to every individual. So, whatever your talent is, it does not surpass sharing the Gospel. THE LORD is no respecter of persons. He wants every nation to repent and accept His salvation (2 Peter 3: 9; 1 Timothy 2: 4).

The Divine gives upon every champion of the Church's spiritual capacities for improving humanity. The Holy Spirit sanctions these gifts to fulfill its divinely ordained functions for the help and encouragement of people. To build up the Church to Spiritual maturity and foster unity of the faith and knowledge of God.

Using their spiritual gifts helps members protect the Church from harmful teaching and build trust and love. No one's gifts are better than anyone else's. Below, I have listed the Scripture of God's gifts; they are as important as speaking in tongues if you have one talent. The list is not exhaustive.

"Word of understanding 1 Corinthians 12: 8, Luke 6: 9, Word of intelligence 1 Corinthians 12: 8, Luke 18: 22, Faith 1 Corinthians 12: 9, Acts 3: 6, Gifts of reviving 1 Corinthians 12: 9, 28; Acts 28: 1-10, Performance of miracles 1 Corinthians 12: 10; Acts 6:8, Prophecy

1 Corinthians 12: 10, 1 Thessalonian 5: 20-21, Ephesians 4: 11, Distinguishing of spirits 1 Corinthians 12:10, Luke 8: 29, Tongues 1 Corinthians 12: 10, Acts 19: 6, Interpretation of tongues (1 Corinthians 12: 10, 14: 13-33), Support 1 Corinthians 12: 28, Administration 1 Corinthians 12: 28, Acts 6: 2-3, Ministry and help Romans 12: 7, 2 Timothy 1: 16-18, Teaching Romans, 12:7; Ephesians 4: 11-14, Encouragement Romans 12: 8, Hebrews 10: 24-25, Giving Romans 12: 8, 1 Corinthians 13: 3, Acts 4: 32-35, Leadership Romans 12: 8, Acts 13: 12, Mercy Romans 12:8, Luke 5: 12-13, Apostleship Ephesians 4: 11, Evangelism Ephesians 4: 11, 2 Timothy 4: 5, Pastoral leadership Ephesians 4: 11, Grace Romans 12: 6, Ephesians 3: 7, 4: 7, 1 Peter 4: 10-11, Readiness to endure persecution 1 Corinthians 13: 3, Intercession Romans 8: 26-27, Hospitality 1 Peter 4: 9, Celibacy 1 Corinthians 7: 8.

ENDNOTES

1 https://www.azquotes.com/quote/866168?ref=church

2 https://www.ucg.org/the-good-news/does-easter-really-commemorate-jesus-christs-resurrection

Milton Keynes UK
Ingram Content Group UK Ltd.
UKHW011928070923
428268UK00003B/25